Be Agile in Life Through AWareness and ACCEptance

Ego Zero™

Awareness. Acceptance. Agility.

egozero.co

Brian Raniewicz and Cindy McMullen

Copyright

Table of Contents

Disclaimer

This publication is for general informational and educational purposes only. It is not intended to be, and should not be relied upon as, a substitute for:

- professional medical or mental health advice, diagnosis, or treatment

- professional legal counsel

- professional financial, investment, or tax advice

Always seek guidance from a licensed physician or other qualified healthcare provider for medical or mental health concerns. For legal or financial matters, consult an appropriately qualified professional.

The authors and publisher have made every reasonable effort to ensure the accuracy of the information provided, but make no guarantees regarding its completeness, accuracy, or relevance to your specific situation. Any reliance you place on the material is at your own risk.

By reading this book, you agree that neither the authors nor the publisher shall be held liable for any loss, injury, or damage, whether direct or consequential, that may result from the use or misuse of this content.

All scenarios, characters, and events are illustrative composites or works of fiction. Any resemblance to real persons, living or dead, or actual events is purely coincidental.

Reading or purchasing this book constitutes your acceptance of these terms.

Dedication

We dedicate this book to Chloe. You were the ultimate AWACCE teacher, and we miss you every day. Kisses, kisses!

Introduction

This book was born from our struggles to understand and practice agility and egolessness in our personal and professional lives.

"Be agile." Does being agile mean I have to follow complicated methods, processes, or use special tools?

"Detach from outcomes." If I detach from outcomes, does that mean I shouldn't care about succeeding or achieving my goals?

"Check your ego at the door." What exactly am I supposed to set aside: my pride, my opinions, my need to be right? How do I let go of these things, especially when they feel so personal?

"Stay focused." How can I do that when my mind feels scattered or overwhelmed?

"Be present." Does being present mean I have to ignore past experiences or stop planning for my future?

"Keep your attention on what's important right now." How do I do that when there are so many distractions competing for my attention?

"Manage distracting thoughts." How do I quiet my mind when my thoughts won't slow down?

"Accept things as they are." Does acceptance mean I'm supposed to live with things I want to change?

If you've struggled with advice about agility and ego that sounds great in theory but feels impossible to apply in real life, you're exactly where you need to be. We wrote this book because we needed practical tools to immediately help us become agile and stop our ego in any situation, from intense work demands and challenging conversations, to managing stress and making better decisions.

In these pages, you'll learn an actionable methodology for becoming truly agile by practicing AWACCE™ (AWareness and ACCEptance) through two practical exercises: Get AWACCE and Be AWACCE. You'll also discover how to overcome your biggest obstacle to being agile, your ego, by using the BRAAD™ exercise.

Thanks for joining us. Let's get started!

How to Use This Book

Study the Framework

Read Chapters 1 to 3 to learn what it means to be AWACCE, what the ego is, how it interferes with your ability to be agile, and the suffering it causes.

Learn the Exercises

Chapter 4 introduces three core exercises: Get AWACCE, Be AWACCE, and BRAAD. Use the AWACCE Daily Tracker to integrate these exercises into your daily life. The supplementary exercises provide additional support.

Apply Exercises in Real Situations

Chapters 5 and 6 demonstrate how to apply the exercises to everyday situations. Refer to these chapters whenever you need practical examples of how to do the Be AWACCE or BRAAD exercises.

Consult the FAQ

Chapter 7 answers common questions and clarifies typical misunderstandings. Check here anytime you feel stuck or confused.

1. BEING AWACCE

AWACCE

Have you ever been so intensely engaged in an experience that time seemed to stop? If so, you've experienced being AWACCE (**pronounced awake**), which stands for **AW**areness and **ACCE**ptance. AWACCE is a state of full attention and zero resistance to the present moment. It is the foundation of being truly agile in life: responsive, adaptable, and in control of your thinking and emotions.

AWACCE has two parts: awareness and acceptance.

Awareness

The first essential element of being AWACCE is awareness. When you're AWACCE, your awareness is extremely strong. You're intensely aware of whatever you've decided to pay attention to in each moment. For example, when you're drinking coffee, you're aware of its taste and warmth. When you're working out, you're aware of how your muscles feel. When you're listening to someone, you're fully aware of what they're saying. When facing a challenging situation, you're fully aware of your emotions, what's happening around you, and how you're responding. Most importantly, your awareness is so intense that your thinking is deliberate and focused.

Other terms for awareness are:

- Being present

- Being focused

- Paying attention

Unless physically unconscious, everyone has some level of awareness. If you're ruminating while sitting in your living room, you're still aware of where you are. If you're worrying about an upcoming meeting while eating, you're still aware that you're eating. However, your awareness isn't intense. You have enough awareness to know what you're doing or what is happening around you, but your awareness isn't strong enough to recognize that your ego is driving you, which we'll explore in Chapters 2 and 3. Sometimes your awareness is so weak that you don't even realize you're thinking.

To be intensely aware, you need something essential: **a focus for every experience**. Every experience consists of a series of moments. Some experiences have only a few moments, like snapping your fingers. Other experiences have many moments, like playing an entire basketball game. At any given moment, there are multiple things you could pay attention to. Having a focus ensures you know exactly what to pay attention to in each moment.

An experience's focus doesn't have to be associated with an action. It can be as simple as being aware and accepting of an experience (i.e., just being present).

Focus directs your attention.

There are two types of focus: stand-alone and supporting. A stand-alone focus isn't associated with a goal. For example, the focus of enjoying time at the park isn't tied to achieving anything else. It stands alone. A supporting focus, on the other hand, is directly connected to achieving a goal. For example, your focus on pitching in a baseball game supports the goal of winning. The focus supports a goal. By having a focus, you prevent unnecessary thinking and emotions related to achieving the goal, enhancing your responsiveness and performance.

Your focus determines precisely what requires your attention in each moment of an experience. Examples include:

- Your surroundings

- Your senses

- Your emotions

- What you say

- What others say

- What you do

- What others do

- What you think

When the focus of an experience requires thinking, you intentionally shift some energy from awareness to your mind. You think only as long as needed, and when thinking is no longer necessary, you stop thinking by intensifying your awareness.

Anything that dulls your awareness, such as junk food, poor sleep, and alcohol, makes it challenging to be AWACCE.

Acceptance

The second essential element of being AWACCE is acceptance. Acceptance is allowing experiences to be as they are. Acceptance prevents mental resistance, making it easier to stay intensely aware. Instead of creating resistance by complaining or judging, you immediately accept. You accept when things go right and when they go wrong. You accept good moments and bad ones. If you make a mistake, you immediately accept it. If someone else makes a mistake, you immediately accept it. If an experience isn't how you expected, you immediately accept it. If someone isn't doing what you think they should be doing, you immediately accept it.

Acceptance allows you to be nimble and responsive to whatever life throws at you. Imagine you're in quicksand. If you resist, you think, "This shouldn't be happening to me!" causing you to react by flailing your arms and screaming, forcing you deeper into the quicksand. Now, imagine you accept being in quicksand. You calmly assess the situation and respond by lying horizontally and slowly moving to safety.

Acceptance doesn't mean avoiding action. When an experience requires a response, you respond. For example, if you're standing in the middle of the street and a bus is heading toward you, you don't say, "I accept that this bus is headed toward me," and then let it hit you. You accept that it's coming, then immediately respond by moving out of the way.

So why aren't you AWACCE all the time? Because of your ego, which we'll explore next.

> *Be agile in life by being AWACCE—*
> *AWareness and ACCEptance.*

2. UNDERSTANDING THE EGO

The Ego

Your ego is the programmed part of your mind. It tells you what to think, feel, and do without you realizing it. Understanding the ego is essential because it is the primary reason being AWACCE, and therefore, being agile, is a struggle. It also causes *a lot* of suffering.

Your ego forms when you lack two skills: intense awareness and acceptance.

When you lack intense awareness, you're unaware of your inner self, the "you" that is conscious aliveness. When you're unaware of your inner self, a void forms around identity, worth, and happiness. To fill the void, society programs you to believe that external things define who you are, what you're worth, and what you need to be happy. These thoughts create egoic identity, egoic worth, and egoic happiness.

1. **Egoic Identity.** Thoughts about external things to define who you are. "My identity is based on external things." Thoughts about external things to define who others are. "Their identity is based on external things."

2. **Egoic Worth.** Thoughts about external things to define your worth. "My worth is based on external things." Thoughts about external things to define others' worth. "Their worth is based on external things."

3. **Egoic Happiness.** Thoughts about external things to define what you need to be happy. "My happiness is based on external things."

When you lack acceptance, you resist what is, what could be, and different points of view. Resistance programs your mind with thoughts about the past, the future, and beliefs. These thoughts create: egoic past and pain, egoic future, and egoic beliefs.

4. **Egoic Past and Pain.** Thoughts and emotions from past experiences you resist because they caused you or others pain. "I can't accept what they did to me."

5. **Egoic Future.** Thoughts about possible future experiences you resist because you fear them. "I can't accept what I fear."

6. **Egoic Beliefs.** Thoughts about life you resist changing because they support a part of your ego, or because it would cause you unhappiness. "I can't accept ideas different from mine."

Because you have an ego, it controls you. Your thinking and emotions are dominated by your ego, causing you to react to situations in ways you wouldn't without ego. Your ego is programmed with so many thoughts that your mind reacts almost nonstop, often without you even noticing. All this thinking keeps your awareness and acceptance weak. So, weak awareness and acceptance create ego, and in turn, ego keeps your awareness and acceptance weak. If you continue to have an ego, you'll continue to suffer and struggle with being agile.

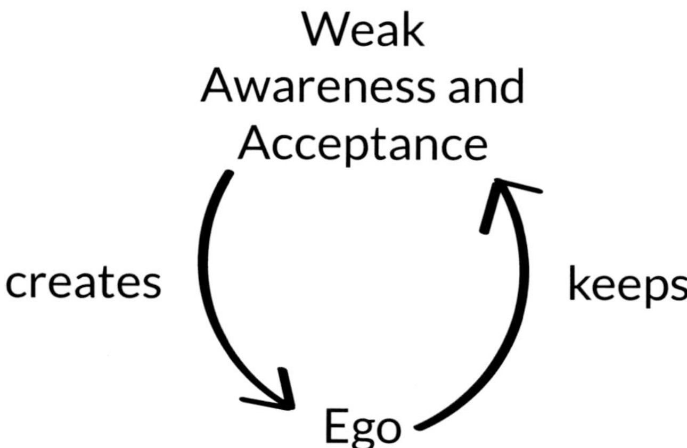

To illustrate the ego in action, let's look at a fictional character named Jack. Jack's ego is made up of these thoughts (in reality, an ego would have many more thoughts):

- Egoic Identity: "I'm a loser."

- Egoic Worth: "I'm worthless."

- Egoic Happiness: "I need money to be happy."

- Egoic Past and Pain: "My childhood was terrible and I'm angry."

- Egoic Future: "My future is bleak. I'm afraid of what's coming."

- Egoic Beliefs: "My political beliefs are right. Anyone who disagrees is dumb."

Jack is on vacation, sitting on a beautiful beach, but his awareness and acceptance are weak. Instead of enjoying his surroundings, his ego takes over. He feels worthless, worries about money, replays painful childhood memories, and fears his future. He picks up his phone and scrolls through social media, judging people with different beliefs.

Suddenly, Jack feels stressed, anxious, and unhappy. His ego ruins his vacation!

Jack's story illustrates what happens when the ego runs wild, an experience many of us have daily.

The ego is weakness disguised as strength.

Activity: Do You Have Ego?

Let's find out. Ask yourself:

- Do you believe people are defined by what they have or do? For example, assuming a job title or a luxury car tells you who someone is.

- Do you believe someone's worth is determined by what they have or do? For example, valuing someone more because of their income or education level.

- Do you believe you need certain things to be happy? For example, a big house, a large salary, or a sports car.

- Do you struggle to accept past experiences? For example, a childhood disappointment or a career setback.

- Do you fear future experiences? For example, losing a job or getting older.

- Do you resist considering other points of view? For example, different political opinions.

You have an ego if you answered "yes" to any of these questions.

Egoic Identity, Worth, and Happiness

Egoic identity, egoic worth, and egoic happiness develop when you're unaware of the inner self. Instead of becoming aware of the inner self, you allow society to program you to believe external things define who you are, what you're worth, and when you're happy. Thoughts act like glue, creating a mental attachment between your mind and external things.

You can use anything external to create identity, worth, or happiness, such as:

- A parent's opinion

- A physical object

- An accomplishment

- An experience

- A belief system

A single external thing can often define all three at once. For example, a job as an investment banker might create:

- Egoic Identity: "I'm an investment banker."

- Egoic Worth: "I'm valuable because I'm an investment banker."

- Egoic Happiness: "I need to be an investment banker to be happy."

Likewise, your egoic identity, worth, and happiness can depend on many external things. For example, your egoic identity of superiority may rely on your clothes, what people think about you, your job title, the size of your home, the kind of car you drive, and how much money you make.

If you lose an external thing linked to your egoic identity, worth, or happiness, your ego won't weaken. As long as you believe, "I need something external to define my identity, worth, and happiness," you'll do one of two things when that external thing is gone:

1. You will seek a different external thing to rebuild the same identity, worth, or happiness. For example, if you think, "I'm better than everyone because I own the most expensive car," you'll trade up when a neighbor buys the same model because you can't handle the impact on your identity, worth, and happiness.

2. You will adopt an entirely new egoic identity, worth, or happiness that still depends on something external. For example, if you think, "I'm worthy because I have a high-paying job," you might switch to "I'm unworthy because I'm unemployed" when you're laid off.

Take back the power from those who control your identity, worth, and happiness!

Egoic Identity

Egoic identity is a mental image of yourself based on something external. You develop egoic identity because society teaches you to believe that external things define you. Instead of knowing your inner self, you create one externally.

You create an egoic identity thought when the thought "I am" combines with a thought about something external, creating a mental attachment between your identity and an external thing.

For example:

- **I am** *an accountant* – merges the thoughts "I am" and "an accountant," creating an identity that depends on your work.

- **I am** *beautiful* – merges the thoughts "I am" and "beautiful," creating an identity that depends on your appearance.

- **I am** *what people say about me* – merges the thoughts "I am" and "what people say about me," creating an identity that depends on people's opinions of you.

- **I am** *a bad person because of what I did* – merges the thoughts "I am" and "a bad person because of what I did," creating an identity based on what you did in the past.

- **I am** *an XYZ member* – merges the thoughts "I am" and "an XYZ member," creating an identity that depends on belonging to a social group.

- **I am** *the conscious self* – merges the thoughts "I am" and "the conscious self," creating an identity based on the concept of the conscious self.

When you believe you're the conscious self, you think about who you are. That's egoic. You want to be aware of who you are, not think about who you are!

The same thing applies to how you see other people or living beings. Instead of being aware of their conscious aliveness, you create a mental image of them based on something external.

For example:

- **He is** *a janitor* – merges the thoughts "He is" and "a janitor," creating an identity of who someone is based on what they do.

- **She is** *ugly* – merges the thoughts "She is" and "ugly," creating an identity of who someone is based on how they look.

- **It is** *a tree* – merges the thoughts "It is" and "a tree," creating an identity of what something is based on a label.

What's the Impact of Egoic Identity?

It creates unnecessary suffering:

- You fear losing your identity. "I'm scared of not being famous anymore!"

- You fear never becoming who you're "supposed to be." "I'm scared of not becoming a star athlete like everyone expects me to."

- You fear expressing yourself because your identity is based on people's judgments of you. "I'm afraid they'll think I'm stupid if they don't like my idea."

- You fear losing your top ranking because you'll no longer be special. "I can't lose my number one ranking because I'll be basic!"

- You feel unhappy if you dislike who you are. "I don't like myself!"

- You buy things to maintain your image, even if you can't afford them. "I need that expensive watch because I want everyone to know I'm wealthy."

- You do certain activities just because "someone like you" is expected to. "I must attend medical school because that's what's expected of me."

- You argue or fight with people who threaten your image. "Back off. You're making me look bad!"

- You justify actions based on your egoic identity. "I'm better than everyone else, so the rules don't apply to me."

- You cheat or lie to protect your image. "I must tell people I'm still working, even though I just got laid off."

- You harm others for "who they are." "I can push you around because you're dumb!"

- You see labels, not aliveness, so life feels dull. "All I see is a tree. Boring."

- You avoid new opportunities that could hurt your image. "I can't start my own business because I could become a failure."

- You limit yourself because of your egoic identity. "I'm a victim, so I can't do anything to help myself."

- You can be manipulated. "The influencer said to give $1,000 because that's what good followers do."

- You stay unaware of who you are, conscious aliveness.

What's the Alternative?

- You are aware of the conscious aliveness in yourself and others.

- You are immune to others' judgments or opinions about who you are because you don't merge anything external with who you are.

- You use labels to communicate, but you know a label is just a thought. You don't use labels as substitutes for being aware of who you or others are.

- You feel the freedom and power of not having to prove who you are.

- You don't experience the suffering of having an egoic identity, like fear, unhappiness, and conflict.

*Stop thinking about who you are and
start being aware of who you are.*

Activity: What External Things Define Who You Are?

Let's find out. Ask yourself:

- What would you be embarrassed or ashamed to lose? For example, your job, money, social status, looks, or a relationship.

- What do you want people to notice about you? For example, your success, beauty, intelligence, strength, or popularity.

- What are you afraid others might think about you? For example, that you're a failure, unattractive, or unimportant.

- What negative labels do you secretly fear describe you? For example, that you're not smart enough, attractive enough, or successful enough.

Your answers are the external things you use to define yourself.

Egoic Worth

Egoic worth is believing you're worthy or unworthy because of something external. You develop egoic worth because society programs you to believe that external things determine your worth. Instead of knowing your inner worth, you create one externally.

You create an egoic worth thought when the thought "I am worthy" or "I am unworthy" merges with a thought about something external, creating a mental attachment between your worth and an external thing.

For example:

- **I am worthy** *because my parents love me* – merges the thoughts "I am worthy" and "because my parents love me," creating worth that depends on your parents continuing to love you.

- **I am unworthy** *because my parents don't love me* – merges the thoughts "I am unworthy" and "because my parents don't love me," creating unworthiness because your parents don't love you.

- **I am worthy** *because I'm wealthy* – merges the thoughts "I am worthy" and "because I'm wealthy," creating worth that depends on having money.

- **I am unworthy** *because I'm poor* – merges the thoughts "I am unworthy" and "because I'm poor," creating unworthiness because you don't have money.

- **I am worthy** *when I win* – merges the thoughts "I am worthy" and "when I win," making worth dependent on winning.

- **I am unworthy** *because I failed* – merges the thoughts "I am unworthy" and "because I failed," creating unworthiness because of a failure.

The same idea applies to other people and living beings. Instead of recognizing their inner worth, you base their worth on something external.

For example:

- **He is unworthy** *because he is uneducated* – merges the thoughts "He is unworthy" and "because he is uneducated," creating unworthiness because of educational level.

- **She is worthy** *because she's the number one salesperson* – merges the thoughts "She is worthy" and "because she's the number one salesperson," creating worthiness because of sales performance.

- **The cockroach is worthless** *because society says so* – merges the thoughts "The cockroach is worthless" and "because society says so," creating unworthiness because of a societal belief.

What's the Impact of Egoic Worth?

It creates unnecessary suffering:

- You fear becoming unworthy. "If I lose my job, I'll be worthless."

- You fear not reaching the goals you believe are needed to be worthy. "I'm scared I won't make partner by 30."

- You feel unhappy when you see yourself as unworthy. "I'm sad because I'm not good enough."

- You don't want friends or family to succeed because it makes you feel like a failure. "I hope he doesn't get that job because I'll feel like a loser!"

- You feel "less" when family, friends, or ex-partners do well. "My ex-wife getting engaged makes me feel worthless!"

- You buy things you can't afford to feel worthy. "These expensive clothes will make me feel valuable."

- You seek approval from people to feel worthy. "Please like me so I can feel good about myself."

- You do activities just to be worthy. "I'm attending medical school because it is a requirement for being worthy in my family."

- You avoid certain activities because you believe you're not worthy enough. "I can't enter that competition because I'm not good enough."

- You avoid opportunities that put your worth at risk. "I can't try out for the team because I might fail and will feel worthless."

- You make failure feel worse by seeing it as "proof" you're unworthy. "That rejection letter proves I'm not good enough."

- You prove others wrong so you can prove your worth. "I must prove my parents wrong to feel good about myself again."

- You argue and fight with people who make you feel unworthy. "You're the worthless one!"

- You want others to feel "less" so you can feel "more." "I write negative comments on people's posts to feel better about myself."

- You cheat, lie, or harm others to protect your worth. "I took credit for the project because I have to be on top to feel good about myself."

What's the Alternative?

- You're aware of your worth and the worth of others, no matter what happens externally.

- You understand that all living beings have conscious aliveness, so all living beings are equally worthy.

- You're immune to others' judgments or opinions about your worth because you don't merge anything external with your worth.

- You keep external things, like a person's looks or skills, separate from a person's worth.

- You recognize that external things have varying worth. The skills associated with performing heart surgery have more economic worth than the skills related to planting flowers. However, you don't associate the monetary value of someone's skill set with their worth.

- You feel the power and freedom of not depending on anything external to feel worthy.

- You don't experience the suffering of having egoic worth, like fear, unhappiness, and conflict.

> *Stop thinking about your worth and*
> *become aware of your inner worth.*

Activity: What External Things Define Your Worth?

Let's find out. Ask yourself:

- What makes you feel valuable, "good enough," or better than others? For example, your career, achievements, intelligence, money, or appearance.

- What would make you feel worthless or "not good enough" if you lost it? For example, a job, a relationship, money, or popularity.

- Whose approval do you need to feel worthy? For example, your parents, friends, boss, partner, or social media followers.

- Which mistakes or failures make you feel like you're "not enough"? For example, losing a job, losing money, or a failed relationship.

- What do you feel you have to do to feel valuable? For example, win arguments, impress people, or achieve more than others.

The external things you named are what you use to define your worth.

Egoic Happiness

Egoic happiness is the dependence on external things to feel happy because either:

- You don't feel your inner happiness (i.e., inner peace), or

- You want relief from unhappiness caused by the ego.

Not all happiness from external things is egoic. If you do something simply because it makes you happy, without expectations about what that happiness will do for you, that's not egoic. But if you expect happiness to fix something inside you or relieve ego-caused unhappiness, that's egoic happiness.

Society determines the external things you desire for happiness.

You create an egoic happiness thought when the thought "I can only be happy" merges with a thought about something external, creating a mental attachment between your happiness and an external thing.

For example:

- **I can only be happy** *if I get married* – merges the thoughts "I can only be happy" and "if I get married." making marriage a requirement for happiness.

- **I can only be happy** *if I make a lot of money* – merges the thoughts "I can only be happy" and "if I make a lot of money," making money a requirement for happiness.

- **I can only be happy** *if I'm skinny* – merges the thoughts "I can only be happy" and "if I'm skinny," making being skinny a requirement for happiness.

- **I can only be happy** *if people like me* – merges the thoughts "I can only be happy" and "if people like me," making other people's favorable opinions a requirement for happiness.

- **I can only be happy** *if I win the championship* – merges the thoughts "I can only be happy" and "if I win the championship," making winning a championship a requirement for happiness.

- **I can only be happy** *if I avoid the past* – merges the thoughts "I can only be happy" and "if I avoid the past," making avoiding the past a requirement for happiness.

- **I can only be happy** *when I think of the good old days* – merges the thoughts "I can only be happy" and "when I think of the good old days," making reminiscing a requirement for happiness.

- **I can only be happy** *when I'm in control* – merges the thoughts "I can only be happy" and "when I'm in control," making being in control a requirement for happiness.

- **I can only be happy** *when things go my way* – merges the thoughts "I can only be happy" and "when things go my way," making things going your way a requirement for happiness.

What's the Impact of Egoic Happiness?

It creates unnecessary suffering:

- You feel constant background emptiness. "Something's always missing."

- You feel unhappy when you don't get the external thing you want. "I can't be happy because I didn't get my ice cream."

- You feel unhappy when you think about happy times ending. "My vacation is ending in five days, so I'm sad now."

- You keep chasing the next thing because external happiness wears off fast. "I'm already planning my next win while the team celebrates this one."

- You feel emptiness even when you achieve. "I got the gold medal, and I still feel empty."

- You need more and more to keep the same level of happiness. "Now I need 10 cookies to be happy."

- You fear losing what makes you happy, even if that happiness has faded. "I rarely play my guitar, yet I'm reluctant to let go of it."

- You feel pressure to be happy around others, even when you're not. "I have a big smile for the selfie, but inside, I'm miserable."

- You buy things just to feel happy, even if you can't afford them. "I have to have it."

- You continue to miss out on your inner happiness.

What's the Alternative?

- You see happiness from external things as temporary, not a replacement for inner happiness, which is always abundant.

- You feel inner happiness no matter what is happening externally.

- You experience external happiness without worrying when it will end. You don't try to hold on to it.

- You enjoy external happiness, but you don't cling to it.

- You don't experience the suffering of having egoic happiness, like emptiness!

Stop chasing happiness and start feel-
ing the happiness within.

Activity: What Do You Rely on for Happiness?

Let's find out. Ask yourself:

- Which achievements do you believe are necessary for happiness? For example, a new job, wealth, success, or fame.

- Which relationships do you believe you must have to feel happy? For example, a soulmate, marriage, or certain friendships.

- What material things do you rely on for happiness? For example, clothes, a car, or luxury items.

- Which future milestones are you waiting for so you can be happy? For example, retirement, moving, financial independence, or a better job.

- What are you afraid of losing because you think you won't be happy without it? For example, a relationship, a job, money, or popularity.

Your answers are the external things you depend on for happiness.

Egoic Past, Pain, Future, and Beliefs

Egoic past and pain, egoic future, and egoic beliefs develop when you lack acceptance. When you resist what is, what was, what could be, or ideas different from yours, you create an attachment to thoughts about the past, the future, and beliefs. You also develop an attachment to emotional pain. You fill your ego with thoughts and emotions about experiences and beliefs you won't accept.

Egoic Past and Pain

Egoic past consists of thoughts about past experiences you don't accept because they caused you or others pain. Egoic past can be from decades ago or seconds ago. Egoic past is unique because it consists of thoughts and pain. Past experiences become egoic past and pain when:

- You resist what you did because you caused yourself or others pain, **creating regret**.

- You resist what others did because they caused you or others pain, **creating resentment.**

Egoic past can become part of egoic identity and worth when you believe that who you are or what you're worth is defined by past experiences.

You create an egoic past thought when the resisting thought, "I regret," or "I resent," merges with a thought about an experience, making a mental attachment to that experience and its pain.

For example:

- **I regret** *that I dropped out of college* – merges the thoughts "I regret" and "that I dropped out of college," creating a mental attachment to the experience of dropping out of college and its pain.

- **I regret** *that I cheated on my partner* – merges the thoughts "I regret" and "that I cheated on my partner," creating a mental attachment to the experience of cheating and its pain.

- **I resent** *being fired unfairly* – merges the thoughts "I resent" and "being fired unfairly," creating a mental attachment to the experience of being fired and its pain.

- **I resent** *my partner spending all our savings* – merges the thoughts "I resent" and "my partner spending all our savings," creating a mental attachment to the experience of losing your savings and its pain.

What's the Impact of Egoic Past and Pain?

It creates unnecessary suffering:

- You torture yourself by replaying negative experiences and feeling the pain over and over. "I keep reliving the events and pain of the breakup."

- You act out in anger, hurting yourself and others. "I keep yelling at my kids because I feel so much anger."

- You engage in violence to get back at those who harmed you. "I slashed his tires because he embarrassed me in the bar."

- You do destructive things to cope with the pain. "I ate a whole pint of ice cream to stop the pain."

- You distance yourself from family and friends. "I didn't attend my sister's wedding because I'm still mad about what she did to me."

- You interpret situations based on the past. "My boss, just like the last one, wants to hold me back."

- You attract negative people and situations. "Every encounter I have is a negative one."

- You block creativity and inspiration. "I can't think of a solution because I'm preoccupied with what my boss said."

- You hurt your performance by focusing on past mistakes. "I missed the free throw because I was ruminating about what that fan said."

What's the Alternative?

- You accept all experiences, good and bad, to prevent becoming attached to them.

- You realize that resisting doesn't change what happened. It just extends the suffering into today and tomorrow.

- You accept, but take action to protect yourself from people who hurt you.

- You accept, but take action to learn and adjust to improve future results.

- You address the consequences of your actions.

- You don't experience the suffering of having egoic past and pain, like engaging in destructive behaviors!

Drop the egoic past and its pain. It's just holding you back.

Activity: Do You Have Egoic Past and Pain?

Let's find out. Ask yourself:

- Is there something from your past you haven't forgiven yourself for? For example, cheating on an exam, quitting a sports team, or ending a relationship poorly.

- Do you replay past mistakes? For example, driving under the influence, missing an investment opportunity, or being mean to a loved one.

- Do you think you're inadequate or unworthy because of something you did? For example, getting divorced, losing a job, or causing harm to someone.

- Are you still angry or bitter about what someone did or didn't do? For example, not helping with college tuition, favoring a sibling, or committing infidelity.

- Do certain situations trigger bigger emotions for you than they should? For example, overreacting when another driver passes you, or becoming angry when someone simply says "no."

- Are you waiting for someone else to apologize so you can feel better? For example, an estranged sibling, a former boss, or an ex-spouse.

If you answered "yes" to any of these, you're holding on to the past. It's time to let go!

Egoic Future

Egoic future is thoughts about "possible" experiences you fear. You fear these experiences because they may cause harm, pain, or unhappiness for you or others. The fear prevents you from accepting the "possible" future experience.

You create an egoic future thought when the resisting thought, "I fear," merges with a thought about the future, making a mental attachment to a future experience.

For example:

- **I fear** *that I might lose my job* – merges the thoughts "I fear" and "that I might lose my job," creating a mental attachment to the possibility of unemployment.

- **I fear** *that my relationship could end* – merges the thoughts "I fear" and "that my relationship could end," creating a mental attachment to the possibility of a breakup.

- **I fear** *that I could get seriously sick* – merges the thoughts "I fear" and "that I could get seriously sick," creating a mental attachment to the possibility of serious illness.

- **I fear** *that I might not have enough money to retire* – merges the thoughts "I fear" and "that I might not have enough money to retire," creating a mental attachment to the possibility of being poor in retirement.

What's the Impact of Egoic Future?

It creates unnecessary suffering:

- You experience constant fear and anxiety. "My stomach knots up whenever I think about next month's bills."

- You experience the pain of something that might not even happen. "Worrying about whether I'll have enough money for retirement makes me sick."

- You make it difficult to face challenges because fear paralyzes you. "I'm afraid to look at my financial situation, even though I know I should."

- You torture yourself by imagining what could happen over and over. "What if this happens? Oh, but what if that happens?"

- You do destructive things, like excessive eating or drinking, to cope with the fear and anxiety. "I drank a whole bottle of wine because I needed something to feel better."

- You block creativity and inspiration because fear and worries push them away. "I can't brainstorm new ideas because I'm worried they won't like what I come up with."

What's the Alternative?

- You address real concerns by making a plan.

- You accept that you can't control everything.

- You realize challenges become problems when the ego gets involved.

- You create space for creative and inspired ideas to form in response to challenges.

- You don't experience the suffering of having egoic future, like constant fear.

Don't worry about the future. Prepare for the future!

Activity: Do You Have Egoic Future?

Let's find out. Ask yourself:

- Are you worrying about things that might never happen? For example, losing a stable job, dying in a plane crash, or your house burning up in flames.

- Do you keep imagining negative scenarios? For example, freezing during an interview, rejection, or losing a loved one.

- Is worrying about the future making it hard for you to enjoy life? For example, checking work email while on vacation, thinking about bills during family time, or losing sleep before a routine doctor visit.

If you answered "yes" to any of these, you're attached to thoughts about the future.

Egoic Beliefs

Egoic beliefs are ideas you refuse to change your mind about. You refuse because they support another part of your ego, or because changing them would force you to do something you don't want to do. Egoic beliefs can be about anything: how to raise children, how people should behave, political ideas, or even how to make pizza! When you have egoic beliefs, you aggressively defend them and refuse to consider other viewpoints.

You create an egoic belief thought when the resisting thought, "I resist changing my mind about," merges with a thought about a belief, making a mental attachment to a belief.

For example:

- **I resist changing my mind about** *my political beliefs* – merges the thoughts "I resist changing my mind about" and "my political beliefs," creating a mental attachment to political beliefs.

- **I resist changing my mind about** *what I eat* – merges the thoughts "I resist changing my mind about" and "what I eat," creating a mental attachment to your food choices.

- **I resist changing my mind about** *how I raise my kids* – merges the thoughts "I resist changing my mind about" and "how I raise my kids," creating a mental attachment to parenting beliefs.

- **I resist changing my mind about** *how I spend my money* – merges the thoughts "I resist changing my mind about" and "how I spend my money," creating a mental attachment to financial habits.

What's the Impact of Egoic Beliefs?

They create unnecessary suffering:

- You end relationships when people don't share your beliefs. "I stopped speaking to my cousin after she changed her political beliefs."

- You justify violence. "I vandalized their shop because I believe that's what bad people deserve."

- You act on outdated or inaccurate beliefs, causing harm or poor results. "I insisted on using a decades-old design, and the new product flopped."

- You resist change, which goes against the natural flow of life. "This is how it's always been and always will be."

- You think you're better than others because of your beliefs. "I look down on people who don't share my political beliefs."

- You can be manipulated by leaders of your belief system. "The guru told me happiness costs $999, so I paid up."

- You stop learning because you're unwilling to hear other points of view. "I refuse to read any book that challenges my thinking."

What's the Alternative?

- You have beliefs, but are open to changing them.

- You share your views without feeling like you must "win" or convince others to believe what you do.

- You listen to others' viewpoints without judgment.

- You don't associate someone's beliefs with their identity or worth.

- You gain knowledge, which helps you be more effective.

- You don't experience the suffering of egoic beliefs, like arguing with everyone!

Drop egoic beliefs to be open to new ideas.

Activity: Do You Have Egoic Beliefs?

Let's find out. Ask yourself:

- Do you hold beliefs because you don't want to give up something? For example, believing fast food is nutritious, so you don't have to give it up.

- Do you refuse to listen when others have different opinions or ideas? For example, not listening to a relative's opinion about immigration because it differs from yours.

- Do you get angry, defensive, or upset when someone challenges your beliefs? For example, getting mad at someone who questions your beliefs about parenting.

- Have you ended or damaged a relationship because someone didn't share your beliefs? For example, ending a friendship because they changed their political views.

If you answered "yes" to any of these, you have egoic beliefs.

Be agile in life by being AWACCE—
AWareness and ACCEptance.

3. WHAT THE EGO DOES

Egoic Cycle

The egoic cycle is an instantaneous chain reaction of thinking, emotions, and actions based on what's in your ego. The activities of the egoic cycle keep your awareness and acceptance weak.

The egoic cycle consists of three egoic activities:

3. **Egoic Thinking**

4. **Egoic Emotion**

5. **Egoic Action**

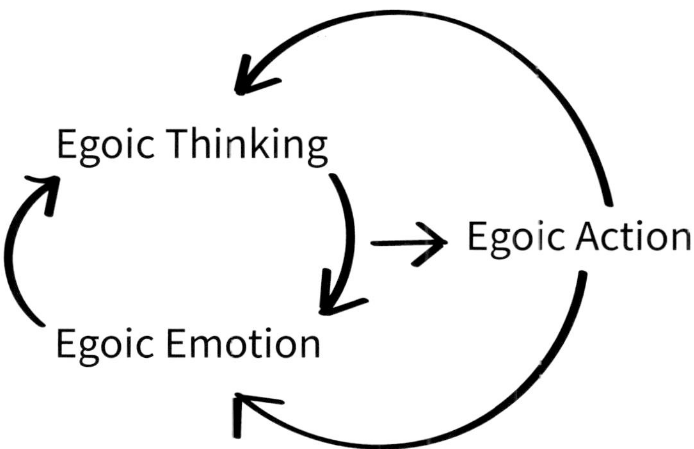

Egoic thinking and emotion trigger each other, and together, they trigger egoic action. Egoic action feeds into egoic thinking and emotions, keeping the cycle running.

In the egoic cycle, you don't have complete control over what you think, feel, and do. You're like a programmed robot: thinking, feeling, and doing based on your ego. You will remain unaware of how the ego influences your thoughts, emotions, and actions until you intensify your awareness and acceptance.

See the Egoic Reactions section of each experience in Chapter 6 for everyday examples of the egoic cycle.

Egoic Thinking

Egoic thinking initiates the egoic cycle. Your mind reacts to what's happening, guided by your ego.

When your boss says, "Try adding more detail here," and you instantly think, "She's criticizing me because I'm not good enough," you're reacting from egoic worth (believing you're not good enough).

When the store is out of your favorite snack and you think, "Nothing ever goes my way," you're reacting from egoic happiness (not getting what you want for happiness).

Egoic thinking can be unintentional or intentional:

1. **Unintentional egoic thinking** occurs automatically, without you choosing to think. It happens when your awareness is very low, allowing your ego to take control. In this state, your mind randomly thinks from the ego. Only the egoic part of the mind is active. This happens in the background, without you realizing it.

2. **Intentional egoic thinking** occurs when you deliberately start thinking with an ego-driven focus. In this state, your awareness is higher, but not high enough to recognize that the ego is controlling your thoughts. The egoless part of your mind is active, but so is the egoic part.

There are many types of egoic thinking, but we'll stick with the big six:

1. **Egoic Complaining**

2. **Egoic Defining**

3. **Egoic Judging**

4. **Egoic Wanting**

5. **Egoic Ruminating**

6. **Egoic Worrying**

What's the Impact of Egoic Thinking?

- You reinforce the ego because egoic thinking is what keeps the ego strong. "I can't stop thinking about being a loser."

- You keep awareness and acceptance weak, the opposite of what you want. "I think about living instead of experiencing living."

- You let egoic thinking affect egoless thinking. "This is the best solution, but what if I mess it up?"

- You allow egoic thinking to undermine your focus, making you less responsive to the moment. "I missed what the client said because I'm replaying an old argument."

- You experience life through thinking instead of awareness, which prevents you from enjoying it. "I'm at the beach but can't stop thinking about work tomorrow."

- You block creativity and innovation. "I have no new ideas."

- You have trouble listening. "Wait, what did you say?"

- You experience unnecessary emotions like fear, sadness, or anger triggered by egoic thinking. "Endless what-ifs make me feel so worried."

- You let egoic thinking influence your actions, which can harm you or others. "I yelled at my partner because of what she said."

- Your mind works constantly. When you need to think intentionally, it's worn out. "I worried so much last night that I couldn't think clearly during my meeting."

- You aren't controlling your mind. It's controlling you.

What's the Alternative?

- You intentionally think without the influence of ego.

- You stop and return to intense awareness and acceptance when you no longer need to think. Contrary to popular egoic belief, not every moment requires thinking!

- You create space for creative, innovative ideas to form.

- You aren't constantly bombarded by emotions, allowing you to think clearly.

- You're in control, even when chaos surrounds you. That is power!

Stop listening to your egoic thoughts. They serve no purpose other than to strengthen the ego (and make you miserable!).

Activity: Do You Experience Egoic Thinking?

Let's find out. Ask yourself:

- Do you think even when there's no reason to do so? For example, rehashing a conversation that ended hours ago.

- Do you notice your thoughts jumping around randomly? For example, shifting from dinner to worries about work to memories from years ago.

- Do your thoughts cause you unnecessary stress, anxiety, anger, or sadness? For example, worrying about criticism you haven't received yet.

- Do you have trouble quieting your mind, even when you want to stop thinking? For example, struggling to fall asleep because your mind keeps racing.

- Do your thoughts make it hard to pay attention to what's happening? For example, missing parts of a conversation because you're preoccupied with your to-do list.

- Do you repeat thoughts about things that aren't helpful or useful? For example, replaying a mistake repeatedly in your mind.

If you answered "yes" to any of these questions, you have experienced egoic thinking.

As mentioned previously, there are six main types of egoic thinking. Let's start with egoic complaining.

Egoic Complaining

Egoic complaining is thinking that results from refusing to accept something that impacts your ego. Something happens, and you immediately think, "This shouldn't be happening!"

Egoic complaining thoughts look like:

- This shouldn't be happening!

- They shouldn't be this way!

- That shouldn't have happened!

- That shouldn't happen!

Egoic complaining is primarily associated with five parts of the ego.

1. **Egoic Identity.** You complain when you lose a desirable egoic identity. "I shouldn't have been fired because now I'm a total loser."

2. **Egoic Worth.** You complain when you feel unworthy. "My date shouldn't have stood me up because now I feel so worthless."

3. **Egoic Happiness.** You complain when you don't get what you want for happiness. "It shouldn't be raining! Now I can't be happy!"

4. **Egoic Past and Pain.** You complain about your regrets. "I shouldn't have been so mean in my marriage." You complain about your resentments. "My parents shouldn't have been so strict when I was a kid."

5.   **Egoic Beliefs.** You complain about people or experiences that don't align with your beliefs. "She shouldn't be raising her kids that way!"

What's the Impact of Egoic Complaining?

- You experience constant frustration because things don't go the way you want. "Everybody is frustrating me!"

- You create anger and frustration, which feed into egoic thinking, making it darker and more harmful. "One minute, I'm slightly annoyed. The next minute, I'm thinking about hurting someone."

- You're less effective at handling challenges because egoless thinking competes with egoic complaining. "Instead of fixing the flat tire, I ranted about it and arrived late."

- You let complaining ruin an entire experience. "I can't stop complaining about the cold soup."

- You allow minor frustrations to turn into dramatic events that can lead to violence. "They cut me off, so I ran into them to send them a message."

What's the Alternative to Egoic Complaining?

- You're responsive to situations, improving the likelihood of desirable outcomes.

- You accept that things won't always go your way, preventing a minor incident from escalating into a major event.

- You accept what's happening but respond when necessary to improve the experience.

- You can talk about what you dislike, but you do it to inform or to release emotion.

- You don't experience the suffering of egoic complaining, like constant frustration.

If you must complain, timebox it to two min-
utes, then accept and move forward.

Activity: Do You Experience Egoic Complaining?

Let's find out. Ask yourself:

- Do you sometimes think something shouldn't be happening? For example, someone saying no to your request.

- Do you make yourself increasingly upset by talking about something that happened? For example, getting more upset when discussing your coworker's mistake.

- Do you talk instead of taking steps to address a challenge? For example, talking for hours about not having enough money instead of creating a budget.

- Do you let minor frustrations ruin an otherwise good experience? For example, not enjoying a family event because your sister-in-law is drunk.

If you answered "yes" to any of these, you have experienced egoic complaining.

Egoic Defining

Egoic defining is thinking about the identity, worth, and happiness of yourself and others. For example, if you're thinking about "who you are", you're thinking about your egoic identity. If you're thinking about not being good enough, you're thinking about your egoic worth. If you're thinking about what you need to be happy, you're thinking about your egoic happiness.

Egoic defining is also the reactive interpretation of situations. You add "your story" to what you're observing, which is based on your egoic past and beliefs.

Finally, egoic defining includes thinking about how people and experiences should be so they align with your egoic beliefs.

Egoic defining thoughts look like the following:

- I am. They are.

- They should be this way.

- I'm worthy or unworthy. They are worthy or unworthy.

- Something external will make me happy.

- My interpretation of the experience is happening.

- This experience should be this way.

Egoic defining is primarily associated with five parts of the ego.

1. **Egoic Identity.** You think about who you are. "I'm a successful executive." You think about who others are. "She's a doctor."

2. **Egoic Worth.** You think about your worth. "I'm worthless because I didn't get that promotion." You think about the worth of others. "He's worthless because he cheats on his wife."

3. **Egoic Happiness.** You think about what will make you happy. "A new relationship will finally make me happy."

4. **Egoic Past and Pain.** You interpret present experiences through past experiences you haven't accepted. "He's disrespecting me, just like my dad always did."

5. **Egoic Beliefs.** You interpret experiences based on your views of life. "I didn't get the job because I'm old." You think about how people or experiences should be. "He shouldn't be so eccentric."

What's the Impact of Egoic Defining?

- You strengthen your ego by reinforcing the belief that thoughts define who you are and your worth. "I'm worthy. I just have to keep believing it."

- You strengthen your ego by reinforcing the belief that external things will make you "forever happy." "Buying the penthouse will make me happy."

- You reinforce attachments to past experiences and beliefs by interpreting everything through them. "My wife is criticizing me because she thinks I'm a loser, just like my mom."

- You feel unhappy when you think about being worthless. "Thinking about being worthless makes me so sad."

- You misinterpret situations by adding your story or your rigid beliefs. "He's not considering my feedback because I'm young."

- You see people based on sexist, racist, or ageist beliefs. "You're old. What do you know?"

- You see the world through labels, making it feel lifeless. "I see the birds, but feel nothing."

- You treat others poorly because you think about them being inferior. "I ignore the cleaning team because they're beneath me."

- You continue to remain unaware of the conscious aliveness in yourself and others.

What's the Alternative to Egoic Defining?

- You use labels to communicate and learn, but you recognize their limitations. Labels don't replace knowing the conscious aliveness within all living beings.

- You don't immediately interpret situations. You remain aware, take in information, and then intentionally reference the past to inform your understanding.

- You remain open-minded and able to hear other opinions that don't align with your own.

- You feel the aliveness of yourself and other living beings.

- You don't experience the suffering of egoic defining, like feeling worthless.

Activity: Do You Experience Egoic Defining?

Let's find out. Ask yourself:

- Do you quickly label yourself or others based on looks, job, or status? For example, immediately thinking, "She's lazy."

- Do you immediately interpret experiences by adding your past story or beliefs? For example, "He's probably lying because that's what my ex-boyfriend did."

- Do you see life through labels rather than experiencing the aliveness around you? For example, sitting in the park and thinking, "This place is boring."

If you answered "yes" to any of these, you have experienced egoic defining.

Egoic Judging

Egoic judging is thinking that immediately labels someone or something as good or bad because of your ego. You experience something and instantly think, "This is bad!" or "This is good!"

Egoic judging thoughts look like:

- This is good/bad.

- They are good/bad.

Egoic judging is primarily associated with four parts of the ego.

1. **Egoic Identity.** You judge people and experiences as good when they improve your image. "He's good because he made me look good in front of everyone." You judge people and experiences as bad when they harm your image. "He's bad because he made me look bad in front of everyone."

2. **Egoic Worth.** You judge people and experiences as good when they make you feel worthy. "This relationship is good because it makes me feel worthy." You judge people and experiences as bad when they make you feel worthless. "The game was

bad because we lost, and now I feel worthless." You judge people and experiences as bad when you want to protect or restore your worth. "Judging you as bad makes me feel better about myself."

3. **Egoic Happiness.** You judge people or experiences as good when they make you happy. "This job is good because it's making me happy." You judge people or experiences as bad when they don't make you happy. "The concert was bad because it didn't give me the happiness I wanted."

4. **Egoic Beliefs.** You judge people and experiences as good when they align with your egoic beliefs. "My daughter is good because she behaves as she should." You judge people and experiences as bad when they don't align with your egoic beliefs. "My son is bad because he doesn't follow our traditions."

What's the Impact of Egoic Judging?

- You create intense emotions, like anger or frustration. "His driving is bad, and it's making me furious."

- You justify hurting others when you judge them as bad. "You're bad, so I'm allowed to be mean to you."

- You limit your ability to respond effectively to experiences because judgments trigger more egoic thinking (like complaining). "This is bad. This shouldn't be happening to me."

What's the Alternative to Egoic Judging?

- You judge when necessary, like judging someone's skills for a job.

- You limit judgment to a single thought, then take responsive action. For example, you think, "This is bad. How can I fix it?"

- You don't experience the suffering of egoic judging, like constant anger!

Contrary to popular egoic belief, not every-thing requires judgment!

Activity: Do You Experience Egoic Judging?

Let's find out. Ask yourself:

- Do you quickly label people or situations as "good" or "bad"? For example, thinking, "He's a bad person."

- Do you justify harmful thoughts or actions after judging someone or something as "bad"? For example, thinking, "She deserves it because she's a bad person."

- Do you immediately judge experiences or people without stopping to understand them? For example, deciding you dislike someone before talking to them.

If you answered "yes" to any of these, you've experienced egoic judging.

Egoic Wanting

Egoic wanting is thinking driven by the desire for external things associated with your ego. You want something to maintain or protect your identity, feel worthy, or feel happy. The "something" can be anything: a physical object like a car, peer validation, attention from social media followers, or even always wanting to be right.

Society strongly influences what you want. Notice the messaging next time you see a commercial. It often targets your identity, worth, and happiness: to be seen as successful, you need this car!

Egoic wanting thoughts look like:

- I want/need/have to have something to achieve, protect, or improve my image.

- I want/need/have to have something to feel worthy or to defend my worth.

- I want/need/have to have something to fill the void inside me.

Egoic wanting is primarily associated with egoic identity, worth, or happiness:

1. **Egoic Identity.** You want something to enhance your image. "I want to win this game so everyone sees me as number one." You want something to protect your image. "I want plastic surgery to keep looking youthful." You want something to improve your image. "I want a more attractive partner to boost my status."

2. **Egoic Worth.** You want something to feel worthy. "I want my parents' approval so I can feel valuable." You want something to protect your worth. "I want that promotion so I can continue feeling good enough."

3. **Egoic Happiness.** You want something that fills a void or replaces unhappiness caused by the ego. "I want a romantic partner so I can finally be happy."

What's the Impact of Egoic Wanting?

- You want to win because you fear losing identity, worth, or happiness. "I need to win or else I won't be the best."

- You experience endless wanting because external happiness inevitably fades. "I won the gold medal. Now what?"

- You overspend because of how much it takes to maintain your image. "My credit cards are maxed out."

- You end relationships when they don't make you happy anymore. "You don't make me happy anymore, so we must break up."

- You think so much about future desires that you fail to enjoy the present. "I won't enjoy life until I retire!"

What's the Alternative to Egoic Wanting?

- You want things because they genuinely serve a purpose.

- You want things because they make you happy, but you don't rely on them to fill an internal void.

- You pursue ambitions for reasons other than egoic identity, worth, or happiness, preventing attachment to outcomes.

- You accept outcomes whether or not you get what you want.

- If you don't get what you want, you may feel disappointed, but feeling your inner happiness makes coping easier.

- You avoid suffering caused by egoic wanting, such as overspending or endless dissatisfaction.

Contrary to popular egoic belief, wanting expensive items isn't inherently egoic.

Activity: Do You Experience Egoic Wanting?

Let's find out. Ask yourself:

- Do you want something to maintain or enhance your image in others' eyes? For example, wanting a prestigious job so that others think highly of you.

- Do you want things so you feel good about yourself? For example, wanting praise from others to feel valuable.

- Do you constantly chase new things because happiness fades quickly? For example, frequently upgrading your phone to regain excitement.

- Do you always think about what's next instead of enjoying the moment? For example, planning your next vacation before finishing the current one.

- Do you want to defend yourself immediately when someone says something you don't like? For example, quickly arguing instead of openly listening to feedback.

If you answered "yes" to any of these, you've experienced egoic wanting.

Egoic Ruminating

Egoic ruminating is thinking about the thoughts that make up your egoic past. You think about regrets (what you did) and resentments (what others did). Egoic ruminating is nonstop, pointless thinking like "I did a bad thing!" or "They made me unhappy!"

Ruminating serves no useful purpose. Does repeatedly thinking about your unhappy childhood change anything? No! All it does is make you and those around you miserable. Worse still, ruminating reinforces your attachment to the past. The more you ruminate, the stronger that attachment grows. It's a self-reinforcing loop.

Ruminating isn't limited to experiences from years ago. It also applies to things that happened seconds ago. Threw an interception in the football game? If you ruminate, you won't learn from it and will lose focus.

Egoic ruminating thoughts look like:

- I did that (and I can't stop thinking about it).

- They did that (and I can't stop thinking about it).

Egoic ruminating is associated with egoic past and pain.

1. **Egoic Past and Pain.** You think repeatedly about things you did (or didn't do). "I keep replaying the mistake I made at work." You think repeatedly about things others did (or didn't do). "I keep thinking about how poorly that guy treated me."

What's the Impact of Egoic Ruminating?

- You experience intense, painful emotions. "Whenever I think about my childhood, I get so upset."

- You lash out emotionally or physically, hurting yourself or others. "After replaying the insult, I punched the wall out of anger."

- You engage in destructive behaviors to cope. "I eat candy every time I remember the sadness of what they did to me."

- You attract negativity. "The more I dwell on problems, the more negativity surrounds me."

- You hurt your focus and performance. "It's hard to concentrate because I keep thinking about what went wrong."

What's the Alternative to Egoic Ruminating?

- You have unhappy experiences, but you don't ruminate about them. Instead:

- You accept what happened, knowing resistance changes nothing.

- You learn from the experience.

- You release the unhappiness through deep breaths (inhale peace, exhale unhappiness) or safe physical movement.

- You give this moment your intense awareness and acceptance.

- You avoid the suffering caused by egoic ruminating.

*Instead of ruminating, learn from the
past to improve your future.*

Activity: Do You Experience Egoic Ruminating?

Let's find out. Ask yourself:

- Do you repeatedly replay past mistakes or arguments? For example, continually thinking about a disagreement.

- Do you frequently feel painful emotions tied to past experiences? For example, feeling embarrassed when you recall a mistake you made years ago.

- Do you relive old hurts or resentments, hoping the past could somehow change? For example, repeatedly imagining an experience with a different outcome.

- Does focusing on the past hurt your ability to enjoy life or perform well? For example, struggling to concentrate at work because your mind is stuck on a mistake you made.

If you answered "yes" to any of these, you've experienced egoic ruminating.

Egoic Worrying

Egoic worrying is thinking about future "possible" experiences you fear. Egoic worrying is nonstop, pointless thinking that doesn't help you address real concerns.

Egoic worrying thoughts look like:

- What if this happens?

- What if that happens?

Egoic worrying is primarily associated with egoic future.

1. **Egoic Future.** You repeatedly think about possible future experiences you fear. "What if I lose my job?"

What's the Impact of Egoic Worrying?

- You create fear, which feeds into more worrying in a self-reinforcing loop. "The possibility of getting laid off is so scary that I can't stop worrying about it."

- You feel paralyzed, which undermines your ability to work effectively. "I stare at the phone instead of calling the client."

- You hurt your performance. "I panicked because I kept worrying about losing, and now I've lost!"

- You pass up opportunities out of fear. "I can't enter that competition because they might laugh at me."

- You suffer the pain of experiences that may never happen. "I'm stressed because I worry constantly about losing all my money, even though there's no reason to."

- You prevent yourself from getting restful sleep, increasing the likelihood of feared outcomes due to fatigue. "I worried all night, and now I can't focus on finishing my painting."

What's the Alternative to Egoic Worrying?

- You address real concerns through planning and focused action. For example, if you're not meeting your sales goals, you put together a plan and execute it instead of worrying.

- You focus only on concerns you can and want to do something about. Otherwise, you let them go.

- You avoid suffering caused by egoic worrying, such as sleep loss or constant stress.

Activity: Do You Experience Egoic Worrying?

Let's find out. Ask yourself:

- Do you anxiously think about events that might never happen? For example, worrying about losing your job when there's no real indication that you will.

- Do your worries make you feel stuck, unable to act, or interfere with what you should do? For example, losing sleep because you can't stop thinking about potential problems at work.

- Do you avoid risks or new things because something might go wrong? For example, turning down a job interview because you're afraid you might fail.

- Does focusing on negative possibilities hurt your performance, concentration, or enjoyment? For example, performing poorly on a task because your mind is preoccupied with what might go wrong.

- Do you constantly ask "What if..." about future situations you can't control? For example, repeatedly thinking, "What if I get sick?" even though you're currently healthy.

If you answered "yes" to any of these, you've experienced egoic worrying.

Egoic Emotion

Egoic emotion is the second stage of the egoic cycle. Egoic thinking creates egoic emotions. If you complain, you feel frustrated. If you think you're worthless, you feel sad. If you ruminate about someone making you feel "small," you feel angry.

Egoic emotions feed into egoic thinking, trapping you in a repeating cycle of thinking and emotions. When you have egoic thinking, egoic emotions will follow.

But that's not all! Egoic pain amplifies egoic emotions. If egoic thinking triggers anger, egoic pain intensifies the anger. If egoic thinking triggers fear, egoic pain intensifies the fear. If egoic thinking triggers sadness, egoic pain intensifies the sadness. Next time you see someone flip out behind the wheel, you're probably witnessing their egoic pain.

What's the Impact of Egoic Emotion?

- Your emotions become disproportionate to what triggered them. "The barista got my order wrong, and suddenly I felt furious."

- You experience constant emotional reactions, sometimes simmering in the background, sometimes exploding outward. "I felt anxious all day and ended up snapping at my coworkers."

- You allow egoic emotions to fuel more egoic thinking, causing your thoughts to spiral downward. "When sadness hits, I think about how I'm not good enough."

- You engage in destructive behaviors, like excessive drinking, drugs, or overeating, to escape difficult emotions. "I drink to numb the pain."

- You let egoic emotions drive harmful actions toward yourself or others. "I got so angry that I slammed the door, cracking it."

- You damage your relationships. "My constant negativity pushes my friends away."

- You attract negativity. "I keep encountering difficult people."

- Your emotional exhaustion hurts your performance. "I'm so emotionally drained that I can't focus."

- You become dependent on intense emotions to feel alive. "I create drama so that I can feel something."

- You seek increasingly intense emotional experiences due to developing a happiness tolerance. "Last week, going to the game was enough. Now I have to gamble on it."

What's the Alternative to Egoic Emotion?

- You realize your thoughts about an experience create emotions, not the experience itself.

- You experience emotions proportionately to the experience that caused them.

- You see emotions as temporary experiences. You accept them as they arrive and as they pass.

- You don't amplify emotions with more thinking. This applies to happiness as well as unhappiness.

- You release unhappy emotions as they arise (or shortly afterward), preventing them from becoming egoic pain.

- You feel greater peace because you're not disturbed by continuous emotional reactions.

How Do I Stop and Release Egoic Emotion?

- Pause and take a few slow breaths, imagining yourself inhaling peace and exhaling unhappiness.

- For intense emotions, do something more physical (but safe!), such as going for a walk. Crying can also help release emotions.

- Avoid thinking during release. Thoughts like "I shouldn't feel this way" block emotional release.

The thoughts you have create the dissatisfaction you feel.

Activity: Do You Experience Egoic Emotion?

Let's find out. Ask yourself:

- Do you feel strong emotions for no apparent reason? For example, suddenly feeling upset or irritated without knowing why.

- Do your emotions seem more intense than the situation deserves? For example, feeling devastated by minor criticism.

- Do you experience emotions almost constantly, even when nothing major is happening? For example, feeling persistently down or irritated on an ordinary day.

- Do you do things, like overeating or drinking, because of your emotions? For example, eating comfort food to soothe anxiety or sadness.

If you answered "yes" to any of these, you've experienced egoic emotion.

Egoic Action

Egoic action is the third stage of the egoic cycle. Egoic actions are what you do when egoic thinking and egoic emotions take over. Egoic actions are reactionary. You're reacting to egoic thoughts and emotions. It's like being "drunk with ego," pushing you to do things you wouldn't do without their influence.

Examples of egoic actions are:

- You argue or fight to protect your image. "Let's step outside and see who the real man is."

- You argue or fight to defend your beliefs. "Say that about my political party again and see what happens."

- You become defensive about feedback to protect your image and worth. "Your feedback doesn't make sense."

- You settle scores to restore your worth. "Take that. Who's the loser now?"

- You sabotage a teammate because their success threatens your worth. "I misplaced her report so she'd miss the deadline."

- You make mistakes because a competitor gets into your ego. "His trash-talk got to me, and I missed the shot."

- You insult others to feel better about yourself. "Nice outfit. Did the thrift store have a sale?"

- You pass on opportunities because you feel worthless. "I can't pursue my dream of being a baker because I'm not good enough."

- You avoid vulnerability because you fear judgment. "I never express my feelings because I don't want to look weak."

- You're mean to others because you believe they're beneath you. "Get a job, you bum!"

- You maintain your image at all costs. "I get every beauty procedure available because looking old will make me feel worthless."

- You seek constant approval from others. "What do you think of my last post?"

- You engage in behaviors like overeating or drinking to escape egoic thoughts and emotions. "I ate the whole bag of candy because I was so stressed."

What's the Impact of Egoic Action?

- You must work harder because you constantly battle ego-driven distractions.

- You harm your relationships through hurtful or alienating behaviors.

- You experience frequent conflicts due to reactive, impulsive behavior.

- You make poor decisions because your actions stem from egoic thinking and emotions.

- You sabotage your success because ego-driven behavior undermines your goals.

- You suffer financially from impulsive spending to maintain your image or relieve feelings of worthlessness.

- You experience chronic stress and anxiety from the consequences of egoic actions.

- You harm your physical health due to stress, impulsivity, or substance use triggered by egoic emotions.

- You lose credibility and respect due to defensive, aggressive, or dishonest behaviors.

- You damage your professional reputation by resisting feedback or sabotaging colleagues.

- You waste time and energy recovering from mistakes caused by egoic actions, reducing productivity.

- You risk legal trouble from impulsive or aggressive actions (such as fights or reckless driving).

What's the Alternative to Egoic Action?

- You approach challenges with focused thinking, finding creative and practical solutions.

- You openly listen to feedback because constructive criticism doesn't threaten your worth.

- You express yourself confidently without needing to protect your image.

- You respond based on what each moment requires, not driven by your beliefs, judgments, or fears.

- You pursue goals aligned with genuine wants and needs rather than ego.

- You handle conflicts calmly, seeking mutual understanding rather than dominance.

- You pursue opportunities fearlessly, knowing success or failure doesn't define who you are.

- You support others' successes, knowing they don't threaten your worth or identity.

- You achieve professional goals through collaboration and effective decision-making, enhancing your credibility and respect.

- You embrace personal growth by learning from mistakes and failures.

- You avoid suffering the consequences of egoic action.

Stop reacting and start responding!

Activity: Do You Experience Egoic Action?

Let's find out. Ask yourself:

- Do you argue, fight, or insult someone to protect your image, worth, or beliefs? For example, getting defensive when someone disagrees with your opinion.

- Do you hurt someone or secretly hope they fail because their success makes you feel inferior? For example, wishing a coworker won't get promoted because it would make you feel less successful.

- Do you try to "get even" to restore your sense of worth or feel superior? For example, withholding help from someone who criticized you.

- Do you make poor decisions because strong emotions or negative thoughts take control? For example, impulsively quitting a job during a moment of anger.

- Do you do things to fit in, gain approval, or avoid being judged negatively? For example, agreeing with opinions you don't hold so others will like you.

- Do you hold back from trying something new or pursuing an opportunity because you think you're not good enough? For example, turning down a date because you think you're not attractive.

If you answered "yes" to any of these, you've experienced egoic action.

Be agile in life by being AWACCE—
AWareness and ACCEptance.

4. EXERCISES

Overview

Being AWACCE and reducing your ego require two skills:

1. **Intense awareness and acceptance in all situations and**

2. **Stopping the egoic cycle when it begins**

To develop these skills, you will need to practice three foundational exercises daily:

1. **Get AWACCE** – Strengthen your awareness and acceptance.

2. **Be AWACCE** – Maintain awareness and acceptance in all situations.

3. **BRAAD** – Stop the egoic cycle, quickly returning to awareness and acceptance.

Consistent daily practice of these foundational exercises will significantly strengthen your awareness, increase acceptance, and reduce your ego.

Additionally, six exercises can deepen your practice by addressing specific challenges:

1. **Forgive the Past** – Release regrets, resentments, and past pain.

2. **Grieve a Loss** – Process sadness to prevent the formation of egoic past and pain.

3. **Inner Self Awareness** – Increase awareness of your conscious self.

4. **Open to Life** – Overcome regrets, resentments, and losses by opening up to new experiences.

5. **Drop Worries** – Effectively stop egoic worrying as soon as it arises.

6. **No Egoic Thinking** – Quickly recognize and stop egoic thoughts before the egoic cycle begins.

AWACCE Exercises

There are two AWACCE exercises to incorporate regularly throughout your day:

1. **Get AWACCE** – Strengthen your ability to be intensely aware and accepting.

2. **Be AWACCE** – Maintain intense awareness and acceptance during all activities, whether observing, performing tasks, or thinking.

Get AWACCE

What Is It?

Get AWACCE is an exercise to strengthen your awareness and acceptance through breathing.

When Do I Do It?

Do the Get AWACCE exercise periodically throughout your day.

Instructions

1. **Close your eyes.**

2. **Be intensely aware and accepting of the breath in.**

   - Focus on the sensations of air entering your body. Completely accept each sensation.

3. **Be intensely aware and accepting of the breath out.**

   - Focus on the sensations of air leaving your body. Completely accept each sensation.

4. **Repeat steps 2 - 3 two more times.**

   - Do more if desired.

5. **Open your eyes.**

Be AWACCE

What Is It?

Be AWACCE is an exercise that keeps you in intense awareness and acceptance during all experiences. It's easy to be AWACCE in settings where it's comfortable, like a relaxing meditation session. Challenge yourself to also be AWACCE in the wild (i.e., in challenging situations).

Please refer to Chapter 5 for examples of how to apply Be AWACCE in everyday experiences.

When Do I Do It?

All day. Regular practice integrates the AWACCE state into your everyday life.

Instructions

1. **Be aware of your focus from the start of the experience.**

   - Your focus is the main activity or primary aspect of the experience, typically the main action you're doing or the main thing you're attending to. Focus guides what you are aware of (in step 2).

2. **Be intensely aware throughout the experience.**

   - Depending on the focus of the experience and what's happening in the moment, be intensely aware of:

     - Your surroundings

     - Your senses

     - Your emotions, releasing them immediately with a deep breath or something more physical, like exercise

     - What is happening

     - What others are saying

- What you're doing

- If you need to think, return to being intensely aware when thinking is no longer needed.

- If the focus you set in step 1 supports a goal, be sure to give attention to the focus of the experience, not the goal.

3. **Be accepting throughout the experience.**

- Accept the experience as it happens.

  - Accept mistakes.

  - Accept unexpected situations.

  - Accept when others don't behave the way you want.

  - Accept when things don't go as planned.

  - Accept all emotions as you feel them.

  - Refrain from complaining or judging to help with acceptance.

  - Recognize the ego in others to help with acceptance.

  - Recognize that resisting makes the experience worse.

4. **Think only when needed during the experience.**

- Stop thinking periodically by intensifying your awareness so that inspired, creative ideas can form.

- When thinking is no longer necessary, stop it by returning to being intensely aware.

- Examples of experiences that require thinking are:

  - When you speak or communicate ideas.

  - When you address a challenge or solve a problem.

  - When you process information.

BRAAD

What Is It?

BRAAD is an exercise that stops the egoic cycle so you can return to being intensely aware and accepting. Stopping the egoic cycle also weakens the ego.

BRAAD stands for:

- Breathe
- Refocus
- Accept
- Adjust
- Do

At first, BRAAD may feel uncomfortable. For example, if someone honks their horn at you, not giving in to reacting will be challenging. But every time you deny an egoic reaction, the ego weakens.

If you avoid denying egoic reactions in the wild (i.e., in challenging situations), your ego will remain strong. Do BRAAD to return to "Being AWACCE in the Wild."

Please refer to Chapter 6 for examples of how to apply BRAAD in everyday experiences.

When Do I Do It?

Do BRAAD whenever:

- You're not fully aware or accepting.

- You're thinking unnecessarily or struggling with egoic thinking (complaining, labeling, interpreting, judging unnecessarily, wanting for egoic reasons, ruminating, worrying).

- Your emotional reactions are disproportionate to what's happening.

- You're reacting impulsively, defensively, aggressively, or are about to do so.

- You're harming someone or feeling the urge to harm someone.

- You're acting or thinking in ways that don't align with the focus of your current experience.

- You're seeking emotional relief.

Instructions

1. **Breathe.**

    - Take a slow, deep breath with intense awareness.

    - As you inhale, focus on the air entering your nostrils, your lungs expanding, and your chest rising.

    - As you exhale, feel the air leaving your body, your chest lowering, and tension releasing.

2. **Refocus.**

    - Reset your focus.

    - If your focus is egoless, remind yourself of it.

    - If your focus is ego-driven, create a new, egoless one.

        - Your focus is egoic if it's driven by one or more parts of the ego.

    - If you don't have a focus, create an egoless one.

3. **Accept.**

    - Accept the experience.

    - Accept what is happening.

    - Accept how you reacted.

    - Accept what others are doing.

- Recognizing the ego in others helps to accept what they're doing.

4. **Adjust.**

   - Identify adjustments that align your actions with your focus and strengthen your awareness and acceptance. For example:

     - Stop egoic actions.

     - Identify actions that align with your focus.

     - Do additional cycles of Breathe, Refocus, and Accept.

     - Use a more intense activity (e.g., walking) to release remaining emotions fully.

     - Remind yourself to repeat BRAAD if egoic thinking returns.

5. **Do.**

   - Implement the adjustments with intense awareness and acceptance.

AWACCE Daily Tracker

The AWACCE Daily Tracker integrates the **Get AWACCE, Be AWACCE**, and **BRAAD** exercises into your daily routine. You'll practice awareness and acceptance in every experience. Most importantly, you'll become increasingly skilled at spotting and stopping the egoic cycle, moving from noticing your ego after it takes control to catching it the moment it starts. Each time you stop the egoic cycle, your ego weakens.

Here's how it works:

In the morning, you'll fill in the tracker with all the experiences you plan to have for the day, like "Eat Breakfast," "Commute to Work," "Morning Meeting," etc., along with their start and end times. For each experience, you'll also choose a specific focus to direct your attention.

Before each experience begins, you'll review the egoic reactions you noted the last time you tracked this experience. For example, before a staff meeting, you'll review the egoic reactions you had during the previous staff meeting. Being aware of these reactions allows you to stay alert for similar ones and immediately stop the ego when it begins. You'll also do the Get AWACCE exercise before the experience starts, intensifying your awareness and acceptance.

During each experience, you'll do the Be AWACCE exercise. If your ego activates, you'll immediately do the BRAAD exercise to stop it.

After each experience, you'll do the "Was My Ego Active?" questionnaire and record any egoic reactions (e.g., "I complained," "I reacted defensively," "I felt angry") in the Retro: Egoic Activity column. You'll review these notes next time you track the same experience so you can stop the egoic cycle earlier.

AWACCE Daily Tracker Template

Experience	Time	Focus On	Retro: Egoic Activity

Instructions

1. **Start Your Day.**

    - List each experience you'll have today in the "Experience" column, one per row.

    - Write the start and end times for each experience in the "Time" column.

    - In the "Focus On" column, write the specific focus that will guide your attention during each experience.

2. **Before Each Experience.**

    - If you've tracked this experience before, review the "Retro: Egoic Activity" notes from the previous experience.

    - Right before the experience, do the Get AWACCE exercise by taking a couple of deep breaths to intensify your awareness and acceptance.

3. **During Each Experience.**

    - Practice the Be AWACCE exercise throughout the entire experience.

        - Stay aware of your chosen focus.

        - Maintain intense awareness and acceptance.

        - Think intentionally, but only as needed.

        - Stay alert for any of the egoic reactions you noticed last time.

        - If you notice an egoic reaction (thinking, emotions, or actions), immediately do the BRAAD (Breathe, Refocus, Accept, Adjust, Do) exercise to stop it.

4. **After Each Experience.**

- Use the "Was My Ego Active?" questionnaire to determine if your ego was active.

- If your ego was active, update the "Retro: Egoic Activity" column with your identified egoic reactions.

- You'll review these notes before your next similar experience.

Was My Ego Active? Questionnaire

Use this questionnaire after each experience to identify if your ego was active. If it was, update the "Retro: Egoic Activity" column with the applicable statement(s):

- **Complaining: Did you have complaining thoughts?**

  - Write: "I complained about [fill in]."

  - Replace [fill in] with what you complained about (e.g., the cold coffee).

- **Labeling: Did you reactively label people or things?**

  - Write: "I labeled [fill in]."

  - Replace [fill in] with who or what you labeled (e.g., my coworker, other drivers).

- **Interpreting: Did you reactively add "your story" to what happened?**

  - Write: "I reactively believed [fill in]."

  - Replace [fill in] with what you believed (e.g., he didn't like me, she disrespected me).

- **Judging: Did you reactively judge someone or something as good or bad?**

  - Write: "I judged [fill in] as [good/bad]."

  - Replace [fill in] with who or what you judged (e.g., the traffic).

- Replace [good/bad] with either "good" or "bad."

- **Wanting: Did you want something to improve your image or worth, or to fill emptiness?**

  - Write: "I wanted [fill in 1] to [fill in 2]."

  - Replace [fill in 1] with what you wanted (e.g., praise, attention).

  - Replace [fill in 2] with the reason (e.g., feel worthy, look important).

- **Ruminating: Did you repeatedly think about something from the past?**

  - Write: "I ruminated about [fill in]."

  - Replace [fill in] with what you ruminated about (e.g., what my boss said).

- **Worrying: Did you repeatedly think about something in the future?**

  - Write: "I worried about [fill in]."

  - Replace [fill in] with what you worried about (e.g., tomorrow's meeting).

- **Emotions: Did you experience emotions disproportionate to your experience?**

  - Write: "I felt [fill in]."

  - Replace [fill in] with the emotion(s) you felt (e.g., anger, frustration, anxiety).

- **Reacting: Did you react impulsively, become defensive, harm someone, or seek emotional relief?**

  - Write: "I reacted [fill in]."

- Replace [fill in] with what you did (e.g., defensively toward my coworker).

Supplementary Exercises

Forgive the Past

What Is It?

Forgive the Past is an exercise to release regrets, resentments, and painful emotions, whether from today or many years ago. You'll express your thoughts and feelings about these experiences, accept them, and move forward.

You can do this exercise by writing on paper, typing in a journal app, talking openly with someone you trust, or silently reflecting.

One session may be enough, but more painful experiences might require several sessions.

When Do I Do It?

Do this exercise whenever you notice a regret or resentment keeps you stuck and you're ready to move forward.

Instructions

1. **Identify.**

    - Choose a regret or resentment you want to release.

2. **Express.**

    - Describe what happened.

    - Describe the impact it has had on your life.

    - Describe how it made you feel.

    - Don't hold back. Be honest about your thoughts and emotions. Use these prompts if you feel stuck:

        - What happened?

- Why did this experience hurt me?

- How did this experience make me feel?

- How has this affected me?

3. **Release the Pain.**

- Focus intensely on your physical and emotional sensations.

- Breathe deeply, intentionally releasing the pain with each exhale.

- If you want to cry, do it without holding back.

- While releasing the pain, avoid ruminating or judging, as that will block the process.

4. **Accept and Move Forward.**

- Close by saying, "I accept what happened, and I forgive myself and anyone else involved. Forgiveness doesn't mean what happened was okay. It means I'm choosing to move forward, unburdened by the past."

Supplemental Activity

- **Be Creative.**

  - Channel remaining emotions into creative outlets like drawing, painting, writing, music, or physical movement (e.g., dancing or exercise).

  - Use creativity to release and express your emotions directly.

Grieve a Loss

What Is It?

Grieve a Loss is an exercise to process grief from losing someone or something important to you. A loss creates an emotional wound, which sends waves of sadness. To heal, you must fully experience the sadness without getting caught up in thinking, such as complaining or ruminating. Thinking during a wave of sadness prolongs the emotional pain and delays healing.

When Do I Do It?

Do this exercise whenever you experience sadness due to a loss.

Instructions

1. **Be Intensely Aware of the Sadness.**

   - When sadness comes, give it your attention.

   - Don't push it away, ignore it, or distract yourself. Avoiding sadness prevents its release.

   - Observe how it feels without judging or interpreting it.

   - Avoid analyzing, complaining, or mentally replaying the loss.

   - If you start thinking, return your focus to the physical sensation of sadness.

2. **Be Accepting of the Sadness.**

   - Allow yourself to feel sad without resistance.

   - Don't judge yourself or think you "shouldn't" or "don't want to" be sad.

   - Accepting sadness allows it to pass more quickly and thoroughly.

3. **Release the Sadness.**

   - Take a few deep breaths, visualizing each inhale filling you with love and each exhale releasing sadness.

   - You can silently say to yourself, "Inhale love" and "Exhale sadness."

- Repeat this until you feel the wave of sadness begin to fade.

4. **Reconnect with Your Surroundings.**

   - Once the wave of sadness has passed, shift your awareness to your current surroundings or what you're doing.

Supplemental Activities

- **Express Your Feelings Creatively.**

  - If the sadness feels intense or challenging to release, channel it through journaling, art, music, or physical movement (like dance).

- **Physical Release.**

  - Take a short walk or stretch lightly to help release the sadness.

Inner Self Awareness

What Is It?

Inner Self Awareness is an exercise to recognize and reconnect with your inner self, your conscious aliveness. When you connect with your inner self, you become aware of who you are and your worth, and feel your inner happiness.

When Do I Do It?

Do this exercise whenever you want to reconnect with your inner self.

Instructions

1. **Settle In.**

   - Sit comfortably with your back supported, feet flat on the floor, and hands resting comfortably in your lap.

- Take five deep breaths, giving complete attention to each inhale and exhale.

2. **Feel Your Inner Aliveness.**

   - Without analyzing or interpreting, notice the feeling of aliveness inside your body.

   - You might notice sensations like warmth, tingling, energy, or even your heartbeat.

   - Just observe these sensations, feeling your aliveness from within.

3. **Observe the Observer.**

   - Recognize what's been aware throughout this experience, your conscious self.

4. **Close the Experience.**

   - End by giving your attention to three slow breaths.

Open to New Experiences

What Is It?

Open to New Experiences is an exercise to help you reconnect with life by actively engaging in experiences that bring you joy. When you're experiencing grief or working through releasing the past, you might shrink inward, closing yourself off to the world. This exercise helps you reconnect with life.

When Do I Do It?

Do this exercise whenever you feel yourself emotionally withdrawing or closing off, particularly when grieving or letting go of the past.

Instructions

1. **Choose an Activity.**

- Select an activity that brings you joy. It could be as simple as having coffee with a friend, reading a favorite book, volunteering, or walking.

2. **Set Your Focus.**

    - Before you begin, remind yourself to focus on fully engaging in your chosen experience.

3. **Be Intensely Aware.**

    - Give your complete attention to the activity.

    - Notice every detail: the sights, sounds, sensations, and interactions.

4. **Be Accepting.**

    - Accept whatever happens without resistance or judgment.

5. **Reflect Briefly.**

    - After completing the activity, take a moment to notice how you feel, paying special attention to any shifts in openness or mood.

Drop Worries

What Is It?

Drop Worries is an exercise to stop worrying. Either create a plan to address the concern driving the worry or let it go.

When Do I Do It?

Do this exercise whenever you're worrying.

Instructions

1. **Create a Worries and Solutions Grid.**

    - Draw a simple two-column grid. Label the left "Worries" and the right "Solutions."

2. **Identify the Concern Behind the Worry.**

- Write a worry in the left column. For example: "I'm worried about tomorrow's presentation."

3. **Solve It or Drop It.**

- In the right column, write a solution to address your concern. For example: "I'll rehearse my presentation tonight."

- If you cannot do anything or decide it's not worth addressing, write, "Let it go."

4. **Repeat.**

- Repeat steps 2 and 3 until you've addressed all your worries.

5. **Schedule or Act Immediately.**

- Schedule your chosen solutions in your calendar or act immediately.

No Egoic Thinking

What Is It?

No Egoic Thinking is an exercise to prevent the start of the egoic cycle by committing to avoid one type of egoic thinking all day.

There are six types of egoic thinking. You'll select one type to avoid for the day:

1. **No Egoic Complaining**

2. **No Egoic Defining**

3. **No Egoic Judging**

4. **No Egoic Wanting**

5. **No Egoic Ruminating**

6. **No Egoic Worrying**

When Do I Do It?

Do this exercise whenever you want to stop or reduce a specific type of egoic thinking. It's a full-day exercise.

Instructions

1. **Select an Egoic Thinking Type.**

   - In the morning, select one of the six types of egoic thinking you will avoid for the day. For example, "Today I will not engage in egoic complaining."

2. **Intensify Your Awareness When It Starts.**

   - Throughout the day, whenever you notice that type of egoic thinking starting, immediately intensify your awareness. Fully focus your attention on what you're observing or doing.

   - For example, if you're avoiding egoic complaining and feel yourself about to complain about traffic, immediately focus your attention on the details around you (such as cars, buildings, weather).

   - It may also help to briefly remind yourself of your commitment, such as by saying, "I won't complain today."

   Be agile in life by being AWACCE—
   AWareness and ACCEptance.

5. DO BE AWACCE IN EVERYDAY EXPERIENCES

This chapter shows how to apply the Be AWACCE exercise in everyday experiences. The examples provided are intended as a reference rather than content to read straight through. Explore a few situations that resonate with you, and return whenever you need an example of how to apply Be AWACCE in a specific situation.

The specific responses and actions in each scenario are for demonstration only. You decide how you want to respond to your own experiences.

Everyday Routines

You Drink Your Coffee

Be AWACCE, aware and accepting, when drinking coffee.

3. **Aware of the Focus Throughout the Experience.**

   - You're aware of the focus of the experience: to drink coffee.

4. **Intensely Aware Throughout the Experience.**

   - You're intensely aware of the warmth of the cup in your hand, the appearance of the coffee, the aroma, and the taste of the coffee.

5. **Accepting Throughout the Experience.**

   - You accept the experience of drinking coffee by not judging or complaining about the coffee being too hot or bitter.

6. **Think Only When Needed.**

   - You don't think because the experience doesn't require it.

You Eat Breakfast

Be AWACCE, aware and accepting, when eating breakfast.

1. **Aware of the Focus Throughout the Experience.**

   - You're aware of the focus of the experience: to eat breakfast.

2. **Intensely Aware Throughout the Experience.**

   - You're intensely aware of the appearance of your food, the aroma of your food, the taste of your food, and the texture of your food as you chew.

3. **Accepting Throughout the Experience.**

   - You accept the experience of eating breakfast by not judging or complaining about the food being bland or not prepared as you like it.

4. **Think Only When Needed.**

   - You don't think because the experience doesn't require it.

You Wash the Dishes

Be AWACCE, aware and accepting, when washing dishes.

1. **Aware of the Focus Throughout the Experience.**

   - You're aware of the focus of the experience: to wash dishes.

2. **Intensely Aware Throughout the Experience.**

   - You're intensely aware of the warmth of the water on your hands, the soap bubbles on the dishes, the sound of dishes clinking, and the water temperature as you adjust it.

3. **Accepting Throughout the Experience.**

   - You accept the experience by not judging or complaining about the number of dishes or how dirty they are.

4. **Think Only When Needed.**

   - You don't think because the experience doesn't require it.

Leisure and Relaxation

You People Watch

Be AWACCE, aware and accepting, when people-watching.

1. **Aware of the Focus Throughout the Experience.**

   - You're aware of the focus of the experience: to people-watch.

2. **Intensely Aware Throughout the Experience.**

   - You're intensely aware of what people around you are doing, the sounds people are making, body language, and the facial expressions of those nearby.

3. **Accepting Throughout the Experience.**

   - You accept the experience by not judging or complaining about how people look or behave.

4. **Think Only When Needed.**

   - You don't think because the experience doesn't require it.

You Relax at the Park

Be AWACCE, aware and accepting, when at the park.

1. **Aware of the Focus Throughout the Experience.**

   - You're aware of the focus of the experience: to enjoy the park.

2. **Intensely Aware Throughout the Experience.**

- You're intensely aware of trees and plants around you, the warmth of the sun on your skin, and the sounds of birds chirping.

3. **Accepting Throughout the Experience.**

- You accept the experience by not judging or complaining about the weather or noise from other park-goers.

4. **Think Only When Needed.**

- You don't think because the experience doesn't require it.

You Take a Walk

Be AWACCE, aware and accepting, when taking a walk.

1. **Aware of the Focus Throughout the Experience.**

- You're aware of the focus of the experience: to walk.

2. **Intensely Aware Throughout the Experience.**

- You're intensely aware of your surroundings, the scent of fresh air, the sensations in your body as you move, and the sound of your footsteps.

3. **Accepting Throughout the Experience.**

- You accept the experience by not judging or complaining about uneven sidewalks or the humidity level.

4. **Think Only When Needed.**

- You don't think because the experience doesn't require it.

You Work Out

Be AWACCE, aware and accepting, when working out.

1. **Aware of the Focus Throughout the Experience.**

- You're aware of the focus of the experience: to work out.

2. **Intensely Aware Throughout the Experience.**

   - You're intensely aware of how your muscles feel, the sound of your breathing, and your body movements.

3. **Accepting Throughout the Experience.**

   - You accept the experience by not judging or complaining about being tired.

4. **Think Only When Needed.**

   - You think about how to improve your form. You decide on an adjustment and apply it, maintaining intense awareness of your muscles as you adjust your form. Once you're satisfied with the adjustment, you stop thinking by focusing on how your muscles feel.

You Watch a Sunset

Be AWACCE, aware and accepting, when watching a sunset.

1. **Aware of the Focus Throughout the Experience.**

   - You're aware of the focus of the experience: to watch the sunset.

2. **Intensely Aware Throughout the Experience.**

   - You're intensely aware of the changing colors in the sky, the sound of the wind, and the cooler air temperature as the sun sets.

3. **Accepting Throughout the Experience.**

   - You accept the sunset as it is by not judging or complaining about the colors fading too quickly or the temperature becoming cooler.

4. **Think Only When Needed.**

- You don't think because the experience doesn't require it.

You Listen to a Friend

Be AWACCE, aware and accepting, when listening to a friend.

1. **Aware of the Focus Throughout the Experience.**

   - You're aware of the focus of the experience: to listen to your friend.

2. **Intensely Aware Throughout the Experience.**

   - You're intensely aware of what your friend is saying, and your friend's body language and facial expressions

3. **Accepting Throughout the Experience.**

   - You accept what your friend says by not judging or complaining about their opinions or how they express themselves.

4. **Think Only When Needed.**

   - You think of a question to ask your friend. After asking the question, you stop thinking by fully returning your attention to listening.

You Enjoy Vacation

Be AWACCE, aware and accepting, when on vacation.

1. **Aware of the Focus Throughout the Experience.**

   - You're aware of the focus of the experience: to enjoy your vacation.

2. **Intensely Aware Throughout the Experience.**

   - You're intensely aware of the scenery around you, conversations nearby, and how your body feels.

3. **Accepting Throughout the Experience.**

- You accept the vacation as it is by not judging or complaining about delays in activities or crowded locations.

4. Think Only When Needed.

- You think about what you want to do next. After selecting an activity, you stop thinking by intensifying your awareness of the scenery.

Waiting and Delays

You Stand in Line for Pizza

Be AWACCE, aware and accepting, when standing in line for pizza.

1. Aware of the Focus Throughout the Experience. You're aware of the focus of the experience: to wait in line for pizza.

2. Intensely Aware Throughout the Experience. You're intensely aware of what people around you are doing, how your body feels, the sounds of the pizzeria, and the aroma of the pizzas.

3. Accepting Throughout the Experience. You accept the experience by not judging or complaining about the line length or the slow service.

4. Think Only When Needed. You don't think because the experience doesn't require it.

You Wait for the Elevator

Be AWACCE, aware and accepting, when waiting for the elevator.

1. Aware of the Focus Throughout the Experience.

- You're aware of the focus of the experience: to wait for the elevator.

2. Intensely Aware Throughout the Experience.

- You're intensely aware of artwork on the walls, the smell of the elevator lobby, and the sound of elevators moving.

3. **Accepting Throughout the Experience.**

- You accept the experience by not judging or complaining about the elevator taking too long.

4. **Think Only When Needed.**

- You don't think because the experience doesn't require it.

You Wait at the DMV

Be AWACCE, aware and accepting, when waiting at the DMV.

1. **Aware of the Focus Throughout the Experience.**

- You're aware of the focus of the experience: to wait until your number is called at the DMV.

2. **Intensely Aware Throughout the Experience.**

- You're intensely aware of what people around you are doing, announcements being made, and your emotions, releasing them immediately with deep breaths.

3. **Accepting Throughout the Experience.**

- You accept being at the DMV by not judging or complaining about the wait time or the crowded seating area.

4. **Think Only When Needed.**

- You don't think because the experience doesn't require it.

You Get Stuck in Traffic

Be AWACCE, aware and accepting, when stuck in traffic.

1. **Aware of the Focus Throughout the Experience.**

- You're aware of the focus of the experience: to handle being stuck in traffic.

2. **Intensely Aware Throughout the Experience.**

    - You're intensely aware of what the cars around you are doing, and your emotions, releasing them immediately with deep breaths.

3. **Accepting Throughout the Experience.**

    - You accept being in traffic by not judging or complaining about other drivers' actions or how slowly the traffic is moving.

4. **Think Only When Needed.**

    - You think about what to do now that you're late. After texting your boss, you stop thinking by intensifying your awareness of what the cars around you are doing.

Your Flight Gets Delayed

Be AWACCE, aware and accepting, when there's a flight delay.

1. **Aware of the Focus Throughout the Experience.**

    - You're aware of the focus of the experience: to handle the flight delay.

2. **Intensely Aware Throughout the Experience.**

    - You're intensely aware of announcements being made, and your emotions, releasing them immediately with deep breaths.

3. **Accepting Throughout the Experience.**

    - You accept the delay by not judging or complaining about how long the wait is or how it affects your schedule.

4. **Think Only When Needed.**

- You intentionally think about what to do next. You decide to call your husband. After the call, you stop thinking by giving your full attention to a deep breath.

Work and Career

You Give a Presentation

Be AWACCE, aware and accepting, when presenting at work.

1. **Aware of the Focus Throughout the Experience.**

- You're aware of the focus of the experience: to communicate ideas in a presentation.

2. **Intensely Aware Throughout the Experience.**

- You're intensely aware of audience reactions, audience members' questions, and your emotions, releasing them immediately with deep breaths.

3. **Accepting Throughout the Experience.**

- You accept the audience's responses by not judging or complaining about tough questions or their lack of engagement.

4. **Think Only When Needed.**

- You intentionally think while communicating your ideas and when responding to audience questions. After answering each question, you stop thinking by fully returning your attention to the next question. When the presentation is done, you stop all thinking by being intensely aware of a few deep breaths.

You Miss a Deadline

Be AWACCE, aware and accepting, when you've missed a deadline.

1. **Aware of the Focus Throughout the Experience.**

   - You're aware of the focus of the experience: to handle missing a deadline.

2. **Intensely Aware Throughout the Experience.**

   - You're intensely aware of your emotions, releasing them immediately with deep breaths.

3. **Accepting Throughout the Experience.**

   - You accept that you missed the deadline by not judging yourself as bad or complaining about how you shouldn't have missed it.

4. **Think Only When Needed.**

   - You think about what you need to do next. You decide to request an extension. After requesting the extension, you stop thinking by giving your full attention to a deep breath.

Your Boss Gives You Feedback

Be AWACCE, aware and accepting, when receiving feedback.

1. **Aware of the Focus Throughout the Experience.**

   - You're aware of the focus of the experience: to listen to your boss's feedback.

2. **Intensely Aware Throughout the Experience.**

   - You're intensely aware of what your boss is saying, your boss's body language, and your emotions, releasing them immediately with deep breaths.

3. **Accepting Throughout the Experience.**

- You accept the feedback by not judging or complaining about the feedback you disagree with.

4. **Think Only When Needed.**

- You think about the feedback and decide to ask a question. After asking, you stop thinking by returning your full attention to listening. You alternate between asking questions and listening attentively until the feedback session ends. When the feedback meeting is over, you stop all thinking by being intensely aware of a few deep breaths.

You Fix a Coworker's Mistake

Be AWACCE, aware and accepting, when a coworker makes a mistake.

1. **Aware of the Focus Throughout the Experience.**

- You're aware of the focus of the experience: to fix a coworker's mistake.

2. **Intensely Aware Throughout the Experience.**

- You're intensely aware of what your coworker is saying, and your emotions, releasing them immediately with deep breaths.

3. **Accepting Throughout the Experience.**

- You accept your coworker's mistake by not judging your coworker as bad or complaining about the extra work required to fix it.

4. **Think Only When Needed.**

- You think of a solution and tell your coworker. While your coworker applies the solution, you stop thinking and remain intensely aware of your coworker's actions. You alternate between intensely observing and thinking as your coworker encounters challenges. When the fix is completed, you stop all thinking by taking a deep breath.

You Fix Your Own Mistake

Be AWACCE, aware and accepting, when you make a mistake and your boss is mean about it.

1. **Aware of the Focus Throughout the Experience.**

   - You're aware of the focus of the experience: to correct a mistake you made.

2. **Intensely Aware Throughout the Experience.**

   - You're intensely aware of what needs correction, what your boss is saying, and your emotions, releasing them immediately with deep breaths.

3. **Accepting Throughout the Experience.**

   - You accept your mistake and your boss's comments by not judging yourself as bad or complaining about your boss being mean. Recognizing the ego in your boss helps you accept what he's saying.

4. **Think Only When Needed.**

   - You think of a fix. You alternate between being intensely aware and thinking while applying the fix. Once it's fixed, you stop all thinking by giving your full attention to a deep breath.

You Fix a Project

Be AWACCE, aware and accepting, when your project needs fixing.

1. **Aware of the Focus Throughout the Experience.**

    - You're aware of the focus of the experience: to get your project back on track.

2. **Intensely Aware Throughout the Experience.**

    - You're intensely aware of what team members say as they explain the project's issues, and your emotions, releasing them immediately with deep breaths.

3. **Accepting Throughout the Experience.**

    - You accept the project's current state by not judging or complaining about unexpected setbacks or team members' mistakes.

4. **Think Only When Needed.**

    - You think about the changes needed to get the project back on track. After explaining the changes to your team, you alternate between thinking (while answering questions) and intensely listening. Once the meeting ends, you stop all thinking by giving your full attention to a deep breath.

You Prepare for a Sensitive Conversation

Be AWACCE, aware and accepting, when preparing for a sensitive conversation.

1. **Aware of the Focus Throughout the Experience.**

    - You're aware of the focus of the experience: to prepare for a sensitive conversation.

2. **Intensely Aware Throughout the Experience.**

- You're intensely aware of your emotions, releasing them immediately with deep breaths.

3. **Accepting Throughout the Experience.**

   - You accept the need for the sensitive conversation by not judging or complaining about having to have it.

4. **Think Only When Needed.**

   - You think about the points you need to make and practice speaking them. You periodically pause your thinking by focusing on breathing, allowing helpful ideas to form. Once you feel prepared, you stop all thinking by giving your full attention to a deep breath.

You Resolve a Team Conflict

Be AWACCE, aware and accepting, while in a meeting because of a team conflict.

1. **Aware of the Focus Throughout the Experience.**

   - You're aware of the focus of the experience: to resolve the team's conflict.

2. **Intensely Aware Throughout the Experience.**

   - You're intensely aware of what each team member is saying, and your emotions, releasing them immediately with deep breaths.

3. **Accepting Throughout the Experience.**

   - You accept that there's a conflict by not judging or complaining about team members' opinions or the intensity of the discussion.

4. **Think Only When Needed.**

- Throughout the meeting, you alternate between intentional thinking (to process what you're hearing) and intense listening. When the meeting is over, you stop all thinking by being intensely aware of your breathing.

You Solve a Software Bug

Be AWACCE, aware and accepting, when there's a software bug.

1. **Aware of the Focus Throughout the Experience.**

   - You're aware of the focus of the experience: to find and fix a software bug.

2. **Intensely Aware Throughout the Experience.**

   - You're intensely aware of what's written in the error logs, what's happening on-screen as you test, and your emotions, releasing them immediately with deep breaths.

3. **Accepting Throughout the Experience.**

   - You accept that the software has a bug by not judging or complaining about unclear error messages or how long it's taking to fix.

4. **Think Only When Needed.**

   - You think about possible solutions. While reviewing and applying these solutions, you alternate between thinking and intense awareness of your breathing, allowing creative solutions to form. After successfully fixing the bug, you stop all thinking by giving your full attention to a deep breath.

You Fix a Computer Issue

Be AWACCE, aware and accepting, when there's a computer issue.

1. **Aware of the Focus Throughout the Experience.**

- You're aware of the focus of the experience: to fix a computer issue.

2. **Intensely Aware Throughout the Experience.**

   - You're intensely aware of what the computer is doing, and your emotions, releasing them immediately with deep breaths.

3. **Accepting Throughout the Experience.**

   - You accept that the computer isn't working properly by not judging or complaining about the disruption to your work.

4. **Think Only When Needed.**

   - You think of a solution and apply it. You assess if the solution works by closely observing what the computer is doing. You alternate between thinking and intense awareness until the issue is resolved. Once the issue is fixed, you stop all thinking by giving your full attention to a few deep breaths.

You Handle a Bully in a Meeting

Be AWACCE, aware and accepting, when you're in a meeting with a bully.

1. **Aware of the Focus Throughout the Experience.**

   - You're aware of the focus of the experience: to handle a bully dominating the meeting.

2. **Intensely Aware Throughout the Experience.**

   - You're intensely aware of what the bully is saying, the facial expressions of other attendees, and your emotions, releasing them immediately with deep breaths.

3. **Accepting Throughout the Experience.**

- You accept the bully's behavior by not judging him as bad or complaining about how he's dominating the meeting. Recognizing that the bully's dominance and criticism are likely ego-driven helps you accept it.

4. **Think Only When Needed.**

- You think about how to respond effectively. You suggest going around the room to get everyone's input, ensuring everyone can speak uninterrupted. After suggesting this, you stop thinking and fully return to listening and observing.

You Deal with an Angry Customer

Be AWACCE, aware and accepting, when a customer is angry.

1. **Aware of the Focus Throughout the Experience.**

- You're aware of the focus of the experience: to resolve an angry customer's issue.

2. **Intensely Aware Throughout the Experience.**

- You're intensely aware of what the customer is saying, and your emotions, releasing them immediately with deep breaths.

3. **Accepting Throughout the Experience.**

- You accept the experience by not judging the customer as bad or complaining about their anger.

4. **Think Only When Needed.**

- While interacting with the customer, you alternate between thinking of a resolution (thinking) and intense listening (awareness). After resolving the issue, you stop thinking by being intensely aware of a few deep breaths.

Your Coworkers Say Mean Things About Your Weight Gain

Be AWACCE, aware and accepting, when coworkers say mean things about your weight gain.

1. **Aware of the Focus Throughout the Experience.**

    - You're aware of the focus of the experience: handling your coworkers' mean comments about your weight gain.

2. **Intensely Aware Throughout the Experience.**

    - You're intensely aware of what your coworkers are saying, and your emotions, releasing them immediately with deep breaths.

3. **Accepting Throughout the Experience.**

    - You accept your coworkers' comments by not judging them as bad people or complaining about what they said. Recognizing that their ego likely influences them to be mean (to feel more worthy) helps you accept it.

4. **Think Only When Needed.**

    - You think about whether you want to do something about your weight gain. You decide you don't. You stop thinking by giving your full attention to a few deep breaths.

You Contemplate a Career Change

Be AWACCE, aware and accepting, while contemplating a career change.

1. **Aware of the Focus Throughout the Experience.**

    - You're aware of the focus of the experience: to decide on a career change.

2. **Intensely Aware Throughout the Experience.**

- You're intensely aware of your emotions, releasing them immediately with deep breaths.

3. **Accepting Throughout the Experience.**

- You accept that a career decision must be made by not judging or complaining about the difficulty of the decision.

4. **Think Only When Needed.**

- You think about the pros and cons of making a change. At times, you stop thinking completely and shift your attention to breathing, allowing helpful insights to arise.

You Get Laid Off

Be AWACCE, aware and accepting, when you've been laid off.

1. **Aware of the Focus Throughout the Experience.**

- You're aware of the focus of the experience: to figure out your next steps after being laid off.

2. **Intensely Aware Throughout the Experience.**

- You're intensely aware of your emotions, releasing them immediately with deep breaths.

3. **Accepting Throughout the Experience.**

- You accept that you've been laid off by not judging or complaining about the company's decision or your current situation. Recognizing that complaining and judging would make the experience more difficult helps you accept it.

4. **Think Only When Needed.**

- You think about what you need to do to get another job. While writing your plan, you periodically stop thinking by giving your full attention to breathing, allowing insights to arise. Once you've finished your plan, you stop thinking by being intensely aware of a few deep breaths.

Frustrations and Disappointments

You Burn Dinner

Be AWACCE, aware and accepting, when you've burned dinner.

1. **Aware of the Focus Throughout the Experience.**

   - You're aware of the focus of the experience: to deal with a burned dinner.

2. **Intensely Aware Throughout the Experience.**

   - You're intensely aware of the smell of burnt food, smoke, how the burnt food looks, and your emotions, releasing them immediately with deep breaths.

3. **Accepting Throughout the Experience.**

   - You accept that dinner is burned by not judging yourself or complaining about the wasted food.

4. **Think Only When Needed.**

   - You think about what to do next. After deciding to order pizza, you stop thinking by giving your full attention to cleaning the kitchen.

You Receive an Unexpected Bill

Be AWACCE, aware and accepting, when you receive an unexpected bill.

1. **Aware of the Focus Throughout the Experience.**

   - You're aware of the focus of the experience: to handle an unexpected bill.

2. **Intensely Aware Throughout the Experience.**

   - You're intensely aware of the bill details (amount, due date, stated reason), and your emotions, releasing them immediately with deep breaths.

3. **Accepting Throughout the Experience.**

   - You accept the unexpected bill by not judging the company for charging you or complaining about the bill's timing. You recognize that judging and complaining will make the experience worse.

4. **Think Only When Needed.**

   - You think about which expenses you can reduce to cover the bill. After identifying savings and paying the bill, you stop thinking by giving your full attention to a deep breath.

Your Meal Arrives Cold

Be AWACCE, aware and accepting, when your meal is cold.

1. **Aware of the Focus Throughout the Experience.**

   - You're aware of the focus of the experience: to address your cold meal.

2. **Intensely Aware Throughout the Experience.**

   - You're intensely aware of the appearance of your food, your hunger, and your emotions, releasing them immediately with deep breaths.

3. **Accepting Throughout the Experience.**

   - You accept that your meal is cold by not judging or complaining about it. You recognize that judging and complaining will make the experience worse.

4. **Think Only When Needed.**

    - You think about how to address the issue. You decide to speak with the manager. While speaking with the manager, you alternate between expressing your viewpoint (thinking) and listening intensely (awareness). After the conversation, you stop thinking by giving your full attention to a few deep breaths.

You Get Blocked on the Sidewalk

Be AWACCE, aware and accepting, when people block the sidewalk.

1. **Aware of the Focus Throughout the Experience.**

    - You're aware of the focus of the experience: to address people blocking the sidewalk.

2. **Intensely Aware Throughout the Experience.**

    - You're intensely aware of what the people blocking your path are doing, and your emotions, releasing them immediately with deep breaths.

3. **Accepting Throughout the Experience.**

    - You accept the experience by not judging them as bad or complaining about them blocking the sidewalk. Reminding yourself that judging and complaining will make the experience worse helps you to accept.

4. **Think Only When Needed.**

    - You think about what to do, deciding whether to ask them to move or walk around them. After acting, you stop thinking by returning your attention to the experience of walking.

Your Ice Cream Is Melting

Be AWACCE, aware and accepting, when your ice cream is melting in the checkout line.

1. **Aware of the Focus Throughout the Experience.**

    - You're aware of the focus of the experience: to decide what to do about your melting ice cream.

2. **Intensely Aware Throughout the Experience.**

    - You're intensely aware of the person in front of you leaving the checkout line to get another item, the melting ice cream, and your emotions, releasing them immediately with deep breaths.

3. **Accepting Throughout the Experience.**

    - You accept the slow checkout and your melting ice cream by not judging the person ahead of you or complaining about the wait.

4. **Think Only When Needed.**

    - You think about what to do and decide not to act because you believe the wait won't be long, and your ice cream won't melt much more. After deciding, you stop thinking and fully return your attention to observing.

You Get a Bad Haircut

Be AWACCE, aware and accepting, when you get a bad haircut.

1. **Aware of the Focus Throughout the Experience.**

    - You're aware of the focus of the experience: to deal with a bad haircut.

2. **Intensely Aware Throughout the Experience.**

- You're intensely aware of your reflection in the mirror, and your emotions, releasing them immediately with deep breaths.

3. **Accepting Throughout the Experience.**

   - You accept your haircut by not judging how it looks or complaining about the stylist. You recognize that judging and complaining about the haircut won't change it and will only make you feel worse.

4. **Think Only When Needed.**

   - You think about what you can do. You decide to research another stylist with good reviews and call to schedule an appointment. After calling, you stop thinking by being intensely aware of your surroundings.

You Get Beeped At

Be AWACCE, aware and accepting, when someone beeps their car horn at you.

1. **Aware of the Focus Throughout the Experience.**

   - You're aware of the focus of the experience: to handle being beeped at just after the light turns green.

2. **Intensely Aware Throughout the Experience.**

   - You're intensely aware of the sound of the car horn behind you, and your emotions, releasing them immediately with deep breaths.

3. **Accepting Throughout the Experience.**

   - You accept that the driver behind you beeped by not judging them as rude or complaining about their impatience.

4. **Think Only When Needed.**

   - You don't think because the experience doesn't require it.

You Lose a Playoff Game

Be AWACCE, aware and accepting, when you lose a playoff game.

1. **Aware of the Focus Throughout the Experience.**

   - You're aware of the focus of the experience: to process missing the last shot in a basketball game, ending your playoff run.

2. **Intensely Aware Throughout the Experience.**

   - You're intensely aware of what just happened (missing the final shot), and your emotions, releasing them immediately with deep breaths.

3. **Accepting Throughout the Experience.**

   - You accept the missed shot and losing the game by not judging yourself as a bad player or complaining about your teammates' performance. You recognize that judging or complaining won't change what happened; it will only intensify your disappointment.

4. **Think Only When Needed.**

   - You think about what you can do to improve your performance in the next season. Once you're done thinking about what you can improve, you stop all thinking by being intensely aware of your breathing.

You Lose a Gambling Bet

Be AWACCE, aware and accepting, when you lose a bet.

1. **Aware of the Focus Throughout the Experience.**

- You're aware of the focus of the experience: to handle losing a gambling bet.

2. **Intensely Aware Throughout the Experience.**

   - You're intensely aware of your emotions, releasing them immediately with deep breaths.

3. **Accepting Throughout the Experience.**

   - You accept the experience by not judging or complaining about losing the money. You recognize that resisting what happened will only make the experience worse.

4. **Think Only When Needed.**

   - You think about whether you want to gamble again. After making your decision, you stop thinking by being intensely aware of a few deep breaths.

Your Child Misbehaves

Be AWACCE, aware and accepting, when your child is misbehaving.

1. **Aware of the Focus Throughout the Experience.**

   - You're aware of the focus of the experience: to address your child's misbehavior.

2. **Intensely Aware Throughout the Experience.**

   - You're intensely aware of what your child is doing, and your emotions, releasing them immediately with deep breaths.

3. **Accepting Throughout the Experience.**

   - You accept your child's behavior by not judging or complaining about their misbehavior or your parenting.

4. **Think Only When Needed.**

- You think about ways to address your child's behavior. You recall a similar experience with one of your other children and decide to apply what worked then. After responding, you stop thinking by fully returning your attention to observing what your child does now.

Your Parent Says Mean Things

Be AWACCE, aware and accepting, when your parent is mean.

1. **Aware of the Focus Throughout the Experience.**

   - You're aware of the focus of the experience: handling your parent's meanness on the phone.

2. **Intensely Aware Throughout the Experience.**

   - You're intensely aware of what your parent is saying, and your emotions, releasing them immediately with deep breaths.

3. **Accepting Throughout the Experience.**

   - You accept your parents' behavior by not judging your parent as a bad person or complaining about what they said. Recognizing that your parents' meanness is likely ego-driven helps you to accept it.

4. **Think Only When Needed.**

   - You think about how to respond. You decide to tell your parent that the conversation has become negative, and you'll connect with them later. After hanging up, you stop all thinking by being intensely aware of your breathing.

You Disagree with a Friend

Be AWACCE, aware and accepting, when you and your friend disagree.

1. **Aware of the Focus Throughout the Experience.**

   - You're aware of the focus of the experience: to address a disagreement with your friend.

2. **Intensely Aware Throughout the Experience.**

   - You're intensely aware of what your friend is saying, and your emotions, releasing them immediately with deep breaths.

3. **Accepting Throughout the Experience.**

   - You accept your friend's perspective by not judging or complaining about their differing opinions or their communication style.

4. **Think Only When Needed.**

   - You alternate between expressing your viewpoint (thinking), intensely listening (awareness), and processing your friend's viewpoint (thinking), until the disagreement is resolved. Once the disagreement is resolved, you stop all thinking by taking a few deep breaths.

Big Life Moments

Your Wife Says She Wants a Divorce

Be AWACCE, aware and accepting, when your wife says she wants a divorce.

1. **Aware of the Focus Throughout the Experience.**

   - You're aware of the focus of the experience: to process hearing your wife say she wants a divorce.

2. **Intensely Aware Throughout the Experience.**

- You're intensely aware of what your wife is saying, and your emotions, releasing them immediately with deep breaths.

3. **Accepting Throughout the Experience.**

   - You accept the experience by not judging or complaining about her decision. You recognize that resisting her decision will make this painful experience even harder.

4. **Think Only When Needed.**

   - You think about how you want to respond. You decide to go for a walk. You stop all thinking by being intensely aware as you walk.

Your Dog Dies

Be AWACCE, aware and accepting, when your dog dies.

1. **Aware of the Focus Throughout the Experience.**

   - You're aware of the focus of the experience: to process the death of your dog.

2. **Intensely Aware Throughout the Experience.**

   - You're intensely aware of your emotions, releasing them immediately with deep breaths and crying.

3. **Accepting Throughout the Experience.**

   - You accept the experience by not judging or complaining about the death of your dog. You recognize that judging or complaining will only make the experience more painful.

4. **Think Only When Needed.**

   - You think about how you want to handle this moment and decide to spend quiet time alone. After deciding, you stop all thinking by being intensely aware of your breathing.

You Lose a Lot of Money

Be AWACCE, aware and accepting, when you've lost a lot of money.

1. **Aware of the Focus Throughout the Experience.**

   - You're aware of the focus of the experience: to process losing a significant amount of money on an investment.

2. **Intensely Aware Throughout the Experience.**

   - You're intensely aware of your emotions, releasing them immediately with deep breaths.

3. **Accepting Throughout the Experience.**

   - You accept your financial loss by not judging yourself for making the investment or complaining about how unfair it is. Reminding yourself that resisting the loss or complaining will only increase your emotional pain helps you to accept.

4. **Think Only When Needed.**

   - You think about how you'll handle the loss moving forward. You decide that once your emotions have settled, you'll focus on learning how to better identify good investments in the future. You've also decided to go for a walk to help you release your emotions (your next experience). You stop thinking by being intensely aware of a few deep breaths.

Your Friends Move On

Be AWACCE, aware and accepting, when you realize your friends have moved on.

1. **Aware of the Focus Throughout the Experience.**

- You're aware of the focus of the experience: to process realizing that your friends from your 20s have moved on to start families.

2. **Intensely Aware Throughout the Experience.**

   - You're intensely aware of the realization that your friends' lives have changed, and your emotions, releasing them immediately with deep breaths.

3. **Accepting Throughout the Experience.**

   - You accept that your friends have moved into new phases of their lives by not judging their choices or complaining about feeling left behind. You recognize that resisting this change will only cause you greater emotional pain.

4. **Think Only When Needed.**

   - You think about what you can do to establish new social connections. After deciding on a step forward, such as joining groups, attending events, or pursuing new interests, you stop thinking by being intensely aware of your surroundings.

You Attend a High School Reunion

Be AWACCE, aware and accepting, when at your high school reunion.

1. **Aware of the Focus Throughout the Experience.**

   - You're aware of the focus of the experience: to have fun at your high school reunion.

2. **Intensely Aware Throughout the Experience.**

   - You're intensely aware of what your classmates are saying and doing, and of your emotions, releasing them immediately with deep breaths.

3. **Accepting Throughout the Experience.**

   - You accept the experience by not judging or complaining about intrusive questions or comments you disagree with. If someone says something belittling, recognizing it's coming from ego helps you accept it.

4. **Think Only When Needed.**

   - You think about your responses to your classmates' questions. After answering, you stop thinking by fully returning your attention to listening.

News and Social Media

You Watch the News

Be AWACCE, aware and accepting, when watching the news.

1. **Aware of the Focus Throughout the Experience.**

   - You're aware of the focus of the experience: to learn about today's events.

2. **Intensely Aware Throughout the Experience.**

   - You're intensely aware of the images on the TV, what's being said, and your emotions, releasing them immediately with deep breaths.

3. **Accepting Throughout the Experience.**

   - You accept what you're learning by not judging or complaining about the stories they are covering.

4. **Think Only When Needed.**

   - You include brief periods of thinking to evaluate and process the information. When you finish watching, you stop all thinking by being intensely aware of a few deep breaths.

You Scroll Through Social Media

Be AWACCE, aware and accepting, when scrolling social media.

1. **Aware of the Focus Throughout the Experience.**

   - You're aware of the focus of the experience: to be entertained by social media.

2. **Intensely Aware Throughout the Experience.**

   - You're intensely aware of the images in each post, the message of each post, and your emotions, releasing them immediately with deep breaths.

3. **Accepting Throughout the Experience.**

   - You accept what you see in each post by not judging or complaining about differing opinions or the types of posts you encounter.

4. **Think Only When Needed.**

   - You intentionally think about an influencer's recommendation. After deciding, you stop thinking by returning your full attention to the next post.

Be agile in life by being AWACCE—
AWareness and ACCEptance.

6. DO BRAAD TO STOP THE EGO IN EVERYDAY EXPERIENCES

This chapter shows how to apply the BRAAD exercise in everyday experiences. The examples provided are intended as a reference rather than content to read straight through. Explore a few situations that resonate with you, and return whenever you need an example of how to apply BRAAD in a specific situation.

The specific responses and actions in each scenario are for demonstration only. You decide how you want to respond to your own experiences.

Work and Career

You Don't Get the Promotion

Do BRAAD to stop egoic reactions when you find out in a staff meeting that you didn't get promoted.

Egoic Reaction

You associate your identity and worth with your job title. Hearing your colleague got the promotion you wanted triggers egoic thinking.

1. **Egoic Thinking.** You have egoic complaining and defining thoughts like, "I deserved that promotion more than she did. This isn't fair. I worked harder. Now, everyone probably thinks I'm a loser."

2. **Egoic Emotion.** These thoughts trigger anger and egoic pain. The egoic pain intensifies your anger.

3. **Egoic Action.** Driven by your egoic thoughts and emotions, you stop paying attention to the meeting.

Awareness Moment

When you miss an update, you realize your ego is active. You decide to do BRAAD to stop the egoic cycle and become AWACCE.

BRAAD in Action

1. **Breathe.** You take a slow, deep breath to stop the egoic cycle and release your emotions.

2. **Refocus.** You reset your focus to actively participating in the staff meeting.

3. **Accept.** You accept your egoic reaction and that your colleague got the promotion.

4. **Adjust.** You identify adjustments: to actively listen and take notes on the remaining updates, and after the meeting, evaluate why you were passed over so you can take steps to earn the promotion next time.

5. **Do.** You implement these adjustments with intense awareness and acceptance.

Benefits of BRAAD

Doing BRAAD stops the egoic cycle, which:

1. Stops the egoic thinking and anger that interfere with paying attention in the staff meeting.

2. Weakens your ego by not reinforcing that your identity and worth depend on your job title.

3. Strengthens your awareness and acceptance, allowing you to stay engaged during the meeting.

You Make Mistakes During Your Presentation

Do BRAAD to stop egoic reactions when making mistakes during a work presentation.

Egoic Reaction

You associate your identity and worth with others' opinions, so making mistakes during your presentation triggers egoic thinking.

1. **Egoic Thinking.** You have egoic complaining thoughts like, "Ugh, I messed up. Now, everyone probably thinks I'm incompetent."

2. **Egoic Emotion.** These thoughts trigger embarrassment and egoic pain. The egoic pain intensifies your embarrassment.

3. **Egoic Action.** Driven by your egoic thoughts and emotions, you rush your words and make additional mistakes.

Awareness Moment

As you make another mistake, you realize your ego is active. You decide to do BRAAD to stop the egoic cycle and become AWACCE.

BRAAD in Action

1. **Breathe.** You take a slow, deep breath to stop the egoic cycle and release your emotions.

2. **Refocus.** You reset your focus to delivering your presentation.

3. **Accept.** You accept your egoic reaction and the mistakes you've made.

4. **Adjust.** You identify adjustments: to slow down, pause briefly after each key point, and speak clearly.

5. **Do.** You implement these adjustments with intense awareness and acceptance.

Benefits of BRAAD

Doing BRAAD stops the egoic cycle, which:

1. Stops egoic complaining and embarrassment that causes you to make mistakes.

2. Weakens your ego by not reinforcing that your identity and worth depend on others' opinions.

3. Strengthens your awareness and acceptance, allowing you to deliver your presentation effectively.

Your Team Member Calls Out Your Project Delay

Do BRAAD to stop egoic reactions when a team member says your project is behind schedule before it's your turn to give updates in a team meeting.

Egoic Reaction

You associate your identity and worth with your work, so criticism triggers egoic thinking.

1. **Egoic Thinking.** You have egoic wanting and worrying thoughts like, "I need to shut this guy down before everyone thinks I'm incompetent!"

2. **Egoic Emotion.** These thoughts trigger anger. Egoic pain intensifies the anger.

Awareness Moment

As you feel anger rising, you realize your ego is active. You choose to do BRAAD to stop your ego and become AWACCE.

BRAAD in Action

1. **Breathe.** You take a slow, deep breath to stop the egoic cycle and release your emotions.

2. **Refocus.** You reset your focus to giving and receiving updates.

3. **Accept.** You accept your egoic reaction and what your team member did.

4. **Adjust.** You identify an adjustment: to let everyone know that fixes are already in place to get your project back on schedule.

5. **Do.** You implement these adjustments with intense awareness and acceptance.

Benefits of BRAAD

Doing BRAAD stops the egoic cycle, which:

1. Stops the egoic thinking and anger that lead to unnecessary suffering.

2. Weakens your ego by not reinforcing that your identity and worth depend on your work.

3. Strengthens your awareness and acceptance, allowing you to stay engaged during team meetings.

You Get Defensive When Your Boss Gives Feedback

Do BRAAD to stop egoic reactions when your boss gives you feedback.

Egoic Reaction

You associate your identity and worth with your work, so receiving feedback triggers egoic thinking.

1. **Egoic Thinking.** You have egoic wanting thoughts like, "I have to defend my work so my boss sees me as capable and competent."

2. **Egoic Emotion.** These thoughts trigger anxiety. Egoic pain intensifies your anxiety.

3. **Egoic Action.** Driven by your egoic thoughts and emotions, you aggressively defend your work.

Awareness Moment

As you defend your work, you realize your ego is active. You decide to do BRAAD to stop the egoic cycle and become AWACCE.

BRAAD in Action

1. **Breathe.** You take a slow, deep breath to stop the egoic cycle and release your emotions.

2. **Refocus.** You reset your focus to listening to your boss's feedback.

3. **Accept.** You accept your egoic reaction and the feedback your boss is providing.

4. **Adjust.** You identify adjustments: to listen, stop arguing, and take notes.

5. **Do.** You implement these adjustments with intense awareness and acceptance.

Benefits of BRAAD

Doing BRAAD stops the egoic cycle, which:

1. Stops the egoic wanting and anxiety that drive you to defend your work aggressively.

2. Weakens your ego by not reinforcing that your identity and worth depend on your work.

3. Strengthens your awareness and acceptance, allowing you to be responsive to feedback.

You're Dismissive Because You're the Boss

Do BRAAD to stop egoic reactions that drive you to react dismissively to an employee's suggestion.

Egoic Reaction

You base your identity and worth on your role as the boss, which carries the egoic belief that you can act dismissively toward employees. Hearing an employee's suggestion triggers egoic thinking.

1. **Egoic Thinking.** You have egoic judging and defining thoughts like, "That suggestion is ridiculous. She's so dumb."

2. **Egoic Emotion.** These thoughts trigger irritation. Egoic pain intensifies your irritation.

3. **Egoic Action.** Driven by your egoic thoughts and emotions, you openly dismiss the employee's suggestion.

Awareness Moment

When you notice the employee's embarrassed expression, you realize your ego is active. You decide to do BRAAD to stop the egoic cycle and become AWACCE.

BRAAD in Action

1. **Breathe.** You take a slow, deep breath to stop the egoic cycle and release your emotions.

2. **Refocus.** You reset your focus to having a productive team meeting.

3. **Accept.** You accept your egoic reaction and that your employee offered a suggestion.

4. **Adjust.** You identify adjustments: to apologize to the employee and discuss the suggestion.

5. **Do.** You implement these adjustments with intense awareness and acceptance.

Benefits of BRAAD

Doing BRAAD stops the egoic cycle, which:

1. Stops the egoic thinking and irritation that drive you to be dismissive toward your employees.

2. Weakens your ego by not reinforcing your egoic identity, egoic worth, and associated egoic belief.

3. Strengthens your awareness and acceptance, allowing you to create a collaborative work environment.

You Talk Yourself Out of Applying for a Promotion

Do BRAAD to stop egoic reactions when applying for a promotion.

Egoic Reaction

You don't believe you're good enough, so thinking about applying for a promotion triggers egoic thinking.

1. **Egoic Thinking.** You have egoic defining thoughts like, "I'm not good enough for this job. There's no way I'll get it."

2. **Egoic Emotion.** These thoughts cause you to feel worthless. Egoic pain intensifies your feelings of worthlessness.

3. **Egoic Action.** Driven by your egoic thoughts and emotions, you don't apply for the job and eat pizza to make yourself feel better.

Awareness Moment

As you eat the pizza, you realize your ego is active. You decide to do BRAAD to stop the egoic cycle and become AWACCE.

BRAAD in Action

1. **Breathe.** You take a slow, deep breath to stop the egoic cycle and release your emotions.

2. **Refocus.** You reset your focus to applying for the job.

3. **Accept.** You accept your egoic reaction.

4. **Adjust.** You identify adjustments: to put the pizza away and start working on your job application.

5. **Do.** You implement these adjustments with intense awareness and acceptance.

Benefits of BRAAD

Doing BRAAD stops the egoic cycle, which:

1. Stops the defining thoughts and feelings of worthlessness that cause you to sabotage your success.

2. Weakens your ego by not reinforcing the belief that you're not good enough.

3. Strengthens your awareness and acceptance, allowing you to pursue career opportunities confidently.

Personal Relationships

You Feel Inadequate Because of Your Friend's Success

Do BRAAD to stop egoic reactions when your friend shares news of his success.

Egoic Reaction

You associate your identity and worth with how well you're doing compared to others, so hearing about your friend's success triggers egoic thinking.

1. **Egoic Thinking.** You have egoic defining and complaining thoughts like, "I'll never be good enough. Why can't I achieve more?"

2. **Egoic Emotion.** These thoughts trigger feelings of inadequacy. Egoic pain intensifies your feelings of inadequacy.

3. **Egoic Action.** Driven by your egoic thoughts and emotions, you make negative comments about your friend's success.

Awareness Moment

As you make a negative comment, you realize your ego is active. You decide to do BRAAD to stop the egoic cycle and become AWACCE.

BRAAD in Action

1. **Breathe.** You take a slow, deep breath to stop the egoic cycle and release your emotions.

2. **Refocus.** You reset your focus to connecting with your friend.

3. **Accept.** You accept your egoic reaction and your friend's success.

4. **Adjust.** You identify adjustments: actively listen and periodically remind yourself to do BRAAD if egoic thinking starts again.

5. **Do.** You implement these adjustments with intense awareness and acceptance.

Benefits of BRAAD

Doing BRAAD stops the egoic cycle, which:

1. Stops the egoic thinking and feelings of inadequacy that drive you to make negative comments.

2. Weakens your ego by not reinforcing that your identity and worth depend on how you compare to others.

3. Strengthens your awareness and acceptance, allowing you to connect with your friend.

You Argue with Your Partner

Do BRAAD to stop egoic reactions when you're disagreeing with your partner.

Egoic Reaction

You have egoic beliefs about how your partner should behave, so when he behaves differently, it triggers egoic thinking.

1. **Egoic Thinking.** You have egoic complaining thoughts like, "He never listens. He shouldn't have done that! Why can't he be the way I want him to be!"

2. **Egoic Emotion.** These thoughts trigger anger. Egoic pain intensifies your anger.

3. **Egoic Action.** Driven by your egoic thoughts and emotions, you start interrupting your partner and raising your voice.

Awareness Moment

As you interrupt your partner, you realize your ego is active. You decide to do BRAAD to stop the egoic cycle and become AWACCE.

BRAAD in Action

1. **Breathe.** You take a slow, deep breath to stop the egoic cycle and release your emotions.

2. **Refocus.** You reset your focus to resolving the disagreement.

3. **Accept.** You accept your egoic reaction and that your partner behaves differently from how you believe he should.

4. **Adjust.** You identify adjustments: listen actively and stop interrupting.

5. **Do.** You implement these adjustments with intense awareness and acceptance.

Benefits of BRAAD

Doing BRAAD stops the egoic cycle, which:

1. Stops the complaining and anger that cause you to interrupt your partner while he's speaking.

2. Weakens your ego by not reinforcing your egoic belief about how your partner should behave.

3. Strengthens your awareness and acceptance, allowing you to resolve the disagreement.

You Argue With Your Friend About Directions

Do BRAAD to stop egoic reactions while discussing directions with a friend.

Egoic Reaction

You associate your identity and worth with being right, so your friend's disagreement with your directions triggers egoic thinking.

1. **Egoic Thinking.** You have egoic defining and wanting thoughts like, "I'm always right. I must win!"

2. **Egoic Emotion.** These thoughts trigger anger. Egoic pain intensifies your anger.

3. **Egoic Action.** Driven by your egoic thoughts and emotions, you repeatedly interrupt your friend.

Awareness Moment

As you interrupt your friend, you realize your ego is active. You decide to do BRAAD to stop the egoic cycle and become AWACCE.

BRAAD in Action

1. **Breathe.** You take a slow, deep breath to stop the egoic cycle and release your emotions.

2. **Refocus.** You reset your focus to working with your friend to determine the quickest route to the beach.

3. **Accept.** You accept your egoic reaction and that your friend prefers a different route.

4. **Adjust.** You identify adjustments: actively listen to your friend and wait until she finishes speaking to offer your opinion.

5. **Do.** You implement these adjustments with intense awareness and acceptance.

Benefits of BRAAD

Doing BRAAD stops the egoic cycle, which:

1. Stops the egoic thinking and anger that drive you to interrupt your friend repeatedly.

2. Weakens your ego by not reinforcing that your identity and worth depend on being right.

3. Strengthens your awareness and acceptance, allowing you to work with your friend.

You're Afraid You'll Always Be Single

Do BRAAD to stop egoic reactions when you're unhappy being single.

Egoic Reaction

You hold the egoic belief that you must be married to be happy, so being single triggers egoic thinking.

1. **Egoic Thinking.** You have egoic wanting and worrying thoughts like, "I have to get married or I'll never be happy! What if it never happens for me?"

2. **Egoic Emotion.** These thoughts trigger feelings of fear. Egoic pain intensifies your fear.

3. **Egoic Action.** Driven by your egoic thoughts and emotions, you eat a pint of ice cream.

Awareness Moment

As you finish the pint of ice cream, you realize your ego is active. You decide to do BRAAD to stop the egoic cycle and become AWACCE.

BRAAD in Action

1. **Breathe.** You take a slow, deep breath to stop the egoic cycle and release your emotions.

2. **Refocus.** You reset your focus to enjoying the TV show.

3. **Accept.** You accept your egoic reaction and that you're single.

4. **Adjust.** You identify an adjustment: give your full attention to enjoying the TV show.

5. **Do.** You implement this adjustment with intense awareness and acceptance.

Benefits of BRAAD

Doing BRAAD stops the egoic cycle, which:

1. Stops egoic thinking and fear that cause unnecessary suffering about being single.

2. Weakens your ego by not reinforcing the belief that marriage is a requirement for happiness.

3. Strengthens your awareness and acceptance, allowing you to feel inner happiness.

You Think Your Boyfriend Is Cheating

Do BRAAD to stop egoic reactions when your boyfriend texts that he'll be home late.

Egoic Reaction

You haven't accepted that a previous partner cheated, so your boyfriend texting that he'll be late triggers egoic thinking.

1. **Egoic Thinking.** You have egoic defining thoughts like, "He's probably cheating, just like my ex-boyfriend did."

2. **Egoic Emotion.** These thoughts trigger fear. Egoic pain intensifies the fear.

3. **Egoic Action.** Driven by your egoic thoughts and emotions, you start typing an accusatory text message.

Awareness Moment

As you begin typing, you realize your ego is active. You decide to do BRAAD to stop the egoic cycle and become AWACCE.

BRAAD in Action

1. **Breathe.** You take a slow, deep breath to stop the egoic cycle and release your emotions.

2. **Refocus.** You reset your focus to reading your magazine.

3. **Accept.** You accept your egoic reaction and the fact that your boyfriend is coming home late.

4. **Adjust.** You identify adjustments: delete the text, return to reading your magazine, and schedule time tomorrow to do the Forgive the Past exercise.

5. **Do.** You implement these adjustments with intense awareness and acceptance.

Benefits of BRAAD

Doing BRAAD stops the egoic cycle, which:

1. Stops the egoic thinking and fear that cause you to add "your story" to what you're experiencing with your boyfriend.

2. Weakens your ego by not reinforcing thoughts of past relationships.

3. Strengthens your awareness and acceptance, allowing you to assess experiences objectively.

Social Situations

You're About to Fight Someone at a Bar

Do BRAAD to stop egoic reactions when out with friends in a bar, and a man asks you to move.

Egoic Reaction

You associate your identity and worth with appearing strong, so being asked to move triggers egoic thinking.

1. **Egoic Thinking.** You have egoic wanting and worrying thoughts like, "I have to win this confrontation! I need

everyone to see I'm not weak. What will they think if I back down?"

2. **Egoic Emotion.** These thoughts trigger anger. Egoic pain intensifies your anger.

3. **Egoic Action.** Driven by your egoic thoughts and emotions, you insult the man.

Awareness Moment

As you insult the man, you realize your ego is active. You decide to do BRAAD to stop the egoic cycle and become AWACCE.

BRAAD in Action

1. **Breathe.** You take a slow, deep breath to stop the egoic cycle and release your emotions.

2. **Refocus.** You reset your focus to enjoying being with my friends.

3. **Accept.** You accept your egoic reaction and the fact that the man asked you to move.

4. **Adjust.** You identify adjustments: apologize, move since there's enough space, and return to enjoying your time with friends.

5. **Do.** You implement these adjustments with intense awareness and acceptance.

Benefits of BRAAD

Doing BRAAD stops the egoic cycle, which:

1. Stops the egoic thinking and anger that drive you to be aggressive.

2. Weakens your ego by not reinforcing that your identity and worth depend on appearing strong.

3. Strengthens your awareness and acceptance, allowing you to enjoy being with your friends.

You Feel Judged by a Salesperson

Do BRAAD to stop egoic reactions when a salesperson judges you.

Egoic Reaction

You base your identity and worth on feeling superior to others, so when a salesperson looks down on you, it triggers egoic thinking.

1. **Egoic Thinking.** You have egoic defining thoughts like: "I don't know who he thinks he is. He's just a minimum wage worker."

2. **Egoic Emotion.** These thoughts trigger feelings of superiority.

Awareness Moment

As you start feeling superior, you realize your ego is active. You decide to do BRAAD to stop the egoic cycle and become AWACCE.

BRAAD in Action

1. **Breathe.** You take a slow, deep breath to stop the egoic cycle and release your emotions.

2. **Refocus.** You reset your focus to shopping.

3. **Accept.** You accept your egoic reaction and the salesperson's behavior.

4. **Adjust.** You identify an adjustment: shop at another store.

5. **Do.** You implement this adjustment with intense awareness and acceptance.

Benefits of BRAAD

Doing BRAAD stops the egoic cycle, which:

1. Stops the defining thoughts and feelings of superiority that create unnecessary suffering.

2. Weakens your ego by not reinforcing that your identity and worth depend on feeling superior to others.

3. Strengthens your awareness and acceptance, allowing you not to be impacted by judgment.

You Get Lots of Likes On Your Selfie

Do BRAAD to stop egoic reactions after your selfie gets many likes on social media.

Egoic Reaction

You associate your identity and worth with how attractive others think you are, so receiving lots of likes triggers egoic thinking.

1. **Egoic Thinking.** You have egoic defining thoughts like, "I look amazing. I'm special."

2. **Egoic Emotion.** These thoughts trigger feelings of superiority.

3. **Egoic Action.** Driven by your egoic thoughts and emotions, you repeatedly check your post to see how many more likes you've gotten.

Awareness Moment

As you check for new likes again, you realize your ego is active. You decide to do BRAAD to stop the egoic cycle and become AWACCE.

BRAAD in Action

1. **Breathe.** You take a slow, deep breath to stop the egoic cycle and release your emotions.

2. **Refocus.** You reset your focus to reconnecting with your inner self.

3. **Accept.** You accept your egoic reaction and the positive attention your selfie received.

4. **Adjust.** You identify adjustments: put your phone away and reconnect with your inner self for a few minutes.

5. **Do.** You implement this adjustment with intense awareness and acceptance.

Benefits of BRAAD

Doing BRAAD stops the egoic cycle, which:

1. Stops the egoic defining and feelings of superiority that make you unaware of your inner self.

2. Weakens your ego by not reinforcing that your identity and worth depend on how attractive others think you are.

3. Strengthens your awareness and acceptance, allowing you to reconnect with your inner self.

You Feel Anxious at a Social Event

Do BRAAD to stop egoic reactions when you're at a social event.

Egoic Reaction

You associate your identity and worth with how you compare to others, so being around people you perceive as more interesting triggers egoic thinking.

1. **Egoic Thinking.** You have egoic defining thoughts like, "Everyone here has more to offer than I do. I'm not good enough."

2. **Egoic Emotion.** These thoughts trigger insecurity. Egoic pain intensifies your insecurity.

3. **Egoic Action.** Driven by your egoic thoughts and emotions, you avoid interacting with people.

Awareness Moment

As you start withdrawing from interactions, you realize your ego is active. You decide to do BRAAD to stop the egoic cycle and become AWACCE.

BRAAD in Action

1. **Breathe.** You take a slow, deep breath to stop the egoic cycle and release your emotions.

2. **Refocus.** You reset your focus to engaging with others at the event.

3. **Accept.** You accept your egoic reaction.

4. **Adjust.** You identify adjustments: introduce yourself to someone new and ask them a question to start the conversation.

5. **Do.** You implement these adjustments with intense awareness and acceptance.

Benefits of BRAAD

Doing BRAAD stops the egoic cycle, which:

1. Stops the egoic defining and insecurity that cause you to avoid interacting with others.

2. Weakens your ego by not reinforcing that your identity and worth depend on comparisons.

3. Strengthens your awareness and acceptance, allowing you to engage with others.

You Brag to Impress Your Neighbors

Do BRAAD to stop egoic reactions when interacting with your neighbors.

Egoic Reaction

You base your identity and worth on your neighbors' opinions of you, so interacting with them triggers egoic thinking.

1. **Egoic Thinking.** You have egoic wanting thoughts like, "I need my neighbors to hear about our amazing vacation and my huge promotion."

2. **Egoic Emotion.** These thoughts trigger feelings of desperation.

3. **Egoic Action.** Driven by your egoic thoughts and emotions, you start bragging about your family's recent vacation and job success.

Awareness Moment

As you're bragging, you realize your ego is active. You decide to do BRAAD to stop the egoic cycle and become AWACCE.

BRAAD in Action

1. **Breathe.** You take a slow, deep breath to stop the egoic cycle and release your emotions.

2. **Refocus.** You reset your focus to having genuine conversations with your neighbors.

3. **Accept.** You accept your egoic reaction.

4. **Adjust.** You identify adjustments: stop bragging and actively listen.

5. **Do.** You implement these adjustments with intense awareness and acceptance.

Benefits of BRAAD

Doing BRAAD stops the egoic cycle, which:

1. Stops the egoic thinking and emotions that cause you to brag.

2. Weakens your ego by not reinforcing that your identity and worth depend on your neighbors' opinions.

3. Strengthens your awareness and acceptance, allowing you to connect with your neighbors.

You Avoid Friends After Gaining Weight

Do BRAAD to stop egoic reactions that cause you to avoid seeing friends because you've gained weight.

Egoic Reaction

You base your identity and worth on your appearance, so thinking about your friends seeing you after gaining weight triggers egoic thinking.

1. **Egoic Thinking.** You have egoic defining and worrying thoughts like, "I'm less attractive now. What will my friends think?"

2. **Egoic Emotion.** These thoughts trigger fear. Egoic pain intensifies the fear.

3. **Egoic Action.** Driven by your egoic thoughts and emotions, you tell your friends you're busy and can't meet up.

Awareness Moment

As you feel sadness about not seeing your friends, you realize your ego is active. You decide to do BRAAD to stop the egoic cycle and become AWACCE.

BRAAD in Action

1. **Breathe.** You take a slow, deep breath to stop the egoic cycle and release your emotions.

2. **Refocus.** You reset your focus to decide whether to hang out with your friends.

3. **Accept.** You accept your egoic reaction and that you've gained weight.

4. **Adjust.** You identify an adjustment: tell your friends you'll join them this weekend.

5. **Do.** You implement this adjustment with intense awareness and acceptance.

Benefits of BRAAD

Doing BRAAD stops the egoic cycle, which:

1. Stops the egoic thinking and fear that cause you to avoid friends.

2. Weakens your ego by not reinforcing that your identity and worth depend on your appearance.

3. Strengthens your awareness and acceptance, allowing you to enjoy your friends' company.

You Compare Yourself Negatively on Social Media

Do BRAAD to stop egoic reactions when you're comparing yourself negatively to others on social media.

Egoic Reaction

You base your identity and worth on how your life compares to others, so seeing posts from people whose lives seem better triggers egoic thinking.

1. **Egoic Thinking.** You have egoic defining thoughts like, "My life isn't as exciting as theirs. They're way more successful. I'll never measure up."

2. **Egoic Emotion.** These thoughts cause you to feel insecure. Egoic pain intensifies your insecurity.

3. **Egoic Action.** Driven by your egoic thoughts and emotions, you start writing negative comments on others' posts.

Awareness Moment

As you write another negative comment, you realize your ego is active. You decide to do BRAAD to stop the egoic cycle and become AWACCE.

BRAAD in Action

1. **Breathe.** You take a slow, deep breath to stop the egoic cycle and release your emotions.

2. **Refocus.** You reset your focus to watching entertaining content.

3. **Accept.** You accept your egoic reaction.

4. **Adjust.** You identify adjustments: stop commenting negatively, take another deep breath, and find content you enjoy.

5. **Do.** You implement these adjustments with intense awareness and acceptance.

Benefits of BRAAD

Doing BRAAD stops the egoic cycle, which:

1. Stops the defining thoughts and insecurity driving you to comment negatively.

2. Weakens your ego by not reinforcing that your identity and worth depend on how you compare to others.

3. Strengthens your awareness and acceptance, allowing you to enjoy social media.

You Get a Negative Comment on Social Media

Do BRAAD to stop egoic reactions when someone leaves a negative comment on your social media post.

Egoic Reaction

You base your identity and worth on how others judge you, so reading a negative comment triggers egoic thinking.

1. **Egoic Thinking.** You have egoic defining thoughts like, "She's right. I'm not pretty. I'll never be good enough."

2. **Egoic Emotion.** These thoughts cause you to feel unworthy. Egoic pain intensifies your feelings of unworthiness.

3. **Egoic Action.** Driven by your egoic thoughts and emotions, you keep rereading the negative comment, feeling worse each time.

Awareness Moment

As you sulk, you realize your ego is active. You decide to do BRAAD to stop the egoic cycle and become AWACCE.

BRAAD in Action

1. **Breathe.** You take a slow, deep breath to stop the egoic cycle and release your emotions.

2. **Refocus.** You reset your focus to taking your dog for a walk.

3. **Accept.** You accept your egoic reaction and that someone wrote a negative comment.

4. **Adjust.** You identify adjustments: stop rereading the comment and prepare for your walk.

5. **Do.** You implement these adjustments with intense awareness and acceptance.

Benefits of BRAAD

Doing BRAAD stops the egoic cycle, which:

1. Stops the defining thoughts and feelings of unworthiness that create unnecessary suffering.

2. Weakens your ego by not reinforcing that your identity and worth depend on others' opinions.

3. Strengthens your awareness and acceptance, allowing you to read negative comments without reacting negatively.

Common Frustrations

You Get Cut in Line

Do BRAAD to stop egoic reactions when someone cuts the line before you.

Egoic Reaction

Your happiness depends on being treated fairly, so when someone cuts in line, it triggers egoic thinking.

1. **Egoic Thinking.** You have egoic complaining and judging thoughts like, "Seriously? He just cut the line! That's ridiculous!"

2. **Egoic Emotion.** These thoughts trigger anger. Egoic pain intensifies your anger.

Awareness Moment

As your anger builds, you realize your ego is active. You decide to do BRAAD to stop the egoic cycle and become AWACCE.

BRAAD in Action

1. **Breathe.** You take a slow, deep breath to stop the egoic cycle and release your emotions.

2. **Refocus.** You reset your focus to ordering pizza.

3. **Accept.** You accept your egoic reaction and that someone cut the line.

4. **Adjust.** You identify an adjustment: choosing the pizza you want to eat.

5. **Do.** You implement this adjustment with intense awareness and acceptance.

Benefits of BRAAD

Doing BRAAD stops the egoic cycle, which:

1. Stops the egoic thinking and anger that create unnecessary suffering.

2. Weakens your ego by not reinforcing that your happiness depends on fairness.

3. Strengthens your awareness and acceptance, allowing you to stay calm even when someone cuts the line.

You Lose Your Temper in Traffic

Do BRAAD to stop egoic reactions when you're yelling in traffic.

Egoic Reaction

You have an egoic belief that there shouldn't be traffic, so encountering traffic triggers egoic thinking.

1. **Egoic Thinking.** You have egoic judging and complaining thoughts like, "Traffic is the worst! Why is there always traffic?"

2. **Egoic Emotion.** These thoughts trigger frustration. Egoic pain intensifies your frustration.

3. **Egoic Action.** Driven by your egoic thoughts and emotions, you honk aggressively and yell at other drivers.

Awareness Moment

As you honk aggressively, you realize your ego is active. You decide to do BRAAD to stop the egoic cycle and become AWACCE.

BRAAD in Action

1. **Breathe.** You take a slow, deep breath to stop the egoic cycle and release your emotions.

2. **Refocus.** You reset your focus to driving safely.

3. **Accept.** You accept your egoic reaction and the traffic.

4. **Adjust.** You identify adjustments: stop honking and yelling, and put on relaxing music.

5. **Do.** You implement these adjustments with intense awareness and acceptance.

Benefits of BRAAD

Doing BRAAD stops the egoic cycle, which:

1. Stops the egoic thinking and frustration that cause you to be aggressive in traffic.

2. Weakens your ego by not reinforcing your egoic belief that there shouldn't be traffic.

3. Strengthens your awareness and acceptance, allowing you to drive safely in traffic.

Your Neighbors Play Loud Music

Do BRAAD to stop egoic reactions when your neighbors are playing loud music.

Egoic Reaction

Your happiness depends on having a quiet apartment, so hearing your neighbors' music triggers egoic thinking.

1. **Egoic Thinking.** You have egoic complaining and judging thoughts like, "I shouldn't have to listen to their music! This shouldn't be happening to me! This is bad!"

2. **Egoic Emotion.** These thoughts trigger anger. Egoic pain intensifies your anger.

3. **Egoic Action.** Driven by your egoic thoughts and emotions, you bang on the wall and shout at your neighbors.

Awareness Moment

As you bang on the wall, you realize your ego is active. You decide to do BRAAD to stop the egoic cycle and become AWACCE.

BRAAD in Action

1. **Breathe.** You take a slow, deep breath to stop the egoic cycle and release your emotions.

2. **Refocus.** You reset your focus to asking your neighbors to turn down their music.

3. **Accept.** You accept your egoic reaction and that your neighbors are playing loud music.

4. **Adjust.** You identify an adjustment: asking your neighbors to turn their music down.

5. **Do.** You implement this adjustment with intense awareness and acceptance.

Benefits of BRAAD

Doing BRAAD stops the egoic cycle, which:

1. Stops the egoic thinking and anger that cause you to react aggressively.

2. Weakens your ego by not reinforcing that you can only be happy if your apartment is quiet.

3. Strengthens your awareness and acceptance, allowing you to respond when neighbors play loud music.

You Miss the Breakfast Cutoff

Do BRAAD to stop egoic reactions when breakfast service has just ended at a restaurant.

Egoic Reaction

You have an egoic belief that the customer is always right, triggering egoic thinking when you're denied breakfast.

1. **Egoic Thinking.** You have egoic complaining thoughts like, "This is ridiculous! Breakfast ended two minutes ago! They should still serve me. This is so unfair."

2. **Egoic Emotion.** These thoughts trigger anger. Egoic pain intensifies your anger.

3. **Egoic Action.** Driven by your egoic thoughts and emotions, you say something rude to the employee.

Awareness Moment

As you say something rude, you realize your ego is active. You decide to do BRAAD to stop the egoic cycle and become AWACCE.

BRAAD in Action

1. **Breathe.** You take a slow, deep breath to stop the egoic cycle and release your emotions.

2. **Refocus.** You reset your focus to lunch.

3. **Accept.** You accept your egoic reaction and that breakfast service has ended.

4. **Adjust.** You identify adjustments: stop being rude, apologize to the employee, and choose a lunch meal.

5. **Do.** You implement these adjustments with intense awareness and acceptance.

Benefits of BRAAD

Doing BRAAD stops the egoic cycle, which:

1. Stops your egoic complaining and anger that drive you to be mean.

2. Weakens your ego by not reinforcing your belief that the customer is always right.

3. Strengthens your awareness and acceptance, allowing you to adapt when you don't get what you want.

You Lose Your Dinner Reservation

Do BRAAD to stop egoic reactions when your dinner reservation is canceled because you arrived late.

Egoic Reaction

Your happiness depends on things going your way, so losing your reservation triggers egoic thinking.

1. **Egoic Thinking.** You have egoic complaining thoughts like, "I can't believe this is happening to me. My husband drives so slowly, we're always late."

2. **Egoic Emotion.** These thoughts trigger anger. Egoic pain intensifies your anger.

3. **Egoic Action.** Driven by your egoic thoughts and emotions, you begin criticizing your husband.

Awareness Moment

As you criticize your husband, you realize your ego is active. You decide to do BRAAD to stop the egoic cycle and become AWACCE.

BRAAD in Action

1. **Breathe.** You take a slow, deep breath to stop the egoic cycle and release your emotions.

2. **Refocus.** You reset your focus to enjoying dinner out with your husband.

3. **Accept.** You accept your egoic reaction and that you lost your reservation.

4. **Adjust.** You identify adjustments: stop criticizing your husband and pick another restaurant.

5. **Do.** You implement these adjustments with intense awareness and acceptance.

Benefits of BRAAD

Doing BRAAD stops the egoic cycle, which:

1. Stops the complaining and anger that lead you to criticize your husband.

2. Weakens your ego by not reinforcing that your happiness depends on everything going your way.

3. Strengthens your awareness and acceptance, allowing you to adapt to a change in plans.

Your Family Criticizes Your Life Choices

Do BRAAD to stop egoic reactions when family members disagree with how you live your life.

Egoic Reaction

You base your identity and worth on how you live your life, so criticism from your family triggers egoic thinking.

1. **Egoic Thinking.** You have egoic wanting thoughts like, "I need to defend myself and show them my way is right."

2. **Egoic Emotion.** These thoughts trigger anger. Egoic pain intensifies your anger.

3. **Egoic Action.** Driven by your egoic thoughts and emotions, you insult your family members.

Awareness Moment

As you hear yourself insult your family members, you realize your ego is active. You decide to do BRAAD to stop the egoic cycle and become AWACCE.

BRAAD in Action

1. **Breathe.** You take a slow, deep breath to stop the egoic cycle and release your emotions.

2. **Refocus.** You reset your focus to understanding your family members' perspective.

3. **Accept.** You accept your egoic reaction. Recognizing that your family members' criticism could be driven by ego makes accepting what they're doing easier.

4. **Adjust.** You identify adjustments: stop insulting your family and listen carefully to understand your family's viewpoint.

5. **Do.** You implement these adjustments with intense awareness and acceptance.

Benefits of BRAAD

Doing BRAAD stops the egoic cycle, which:

1. Stops your egoic wanting and anger that drive you to insult your family members.

2. Weakens your ego by not reinforcing that your identity and worth depend on how you live.

3. Strengthens your awareness and acceptance, allowing you to listen to your family members' point of view.

Your Friend Doesn't Say Thank You

Do BRAAD to stop egoic reactions when your friend doesn't thank you for your help.

Egoic Reaction

You have the egoic belief that your help should always be acknowledged, so not receiving a thank you triggers egoic thinking.

1. **Egoic Thinking.** You have egoic complaining thoughts like, "I spent all day helping him, and he couldn't even say thank you! He doesn't appreciate me. What a waste of my time."

2. **Egoic Emotion.** These thoughts trigger frustration. Egoic pain intensifies your frustration.

3.   **Egoic Action.** Driven by your egoic thoughts and emotions, you call your brother to vent about your friend.

Awareness Moment

As you complain to your brother, you realize your ego is active. You decide to do BRAAD to stop the egoic cycle and become AWACCE.

BRAAD in Action

1.   **Breathe.** You take a slow, deep breath to stop the egoic cycle and release your emotions.

2.   **Refocus.** You reset your focus to chatting with your brother about sports.

3.   **Accept.** You accept your egoic reaction and that your friend didn't thank you.

4.   **Adjust.** You identify adjustments: stop venting and shift the conversation to sports.

5.   **Do.** You implement these adjustments with intense awareness and acceptance.

Benefits of BRAAD

Doing BRAAD stops the egoic cycle, which:

1.   Stops the complaining thoughts and frustration that create unnecessary suffering.

2.   Weakens your ego by not reinforcing your belief that your help must always be acknowledged with a thank you.

3.   Strengthens your awareness and acceptance, allowing you to accept others as they are.

Sports

You Throw an Interception in a Football Game

Do BRAAD to stop egoic reactions after throwing an interception during a football game.

Egoic Reaction

You associate your identity and worth with your athletic performance, so making a mistake triggers egoic thinking.

1. **Egoic Thinking.** You have egoic ruminating and defining thoughts like, "I can't believe I did that. Why didn't I wait for the receiver to get open? I'm such an idiot!"

2. **Egoic Emotion.** These thoughts trigger frustration. Egoic pain intensifies your frustration.

3. **Egoic Action.** Driven by your egoic thoughts and emotions, you hesitate on your next play.

Awareness Moment

After getting sacked because you hesitated, you realize your ego is interfering with your performance. You decide to do BRAAD to stop the egoic cycle and become AWACCE.

BRAAD in Action

1. **Breathe.** You take a slow, deep breath to stop the egoic cycle and release your emotions.

2. **Refocus.** You reset your focus to executing each play.

3. **Accept.** You accept your mistakes and your egoic reaction.

4. **Adjust.** You identify adjustments: quickly accept mistakes, learn from them, and decisively execute each play.

5. **Do.** You implement these adjustments with intense awareness and acceptance.

Benefits of BRAAD

Doing BRAAD stops the egoic cycle, which:

1. Stops the egoic thinking and frustration that cause you to hesitate.

2. Weakens your ego by not reinforcing that your identity and worth depend on your athletic performance.

3. Strengthens your awareness and acceptance, allowing you to execute plays to the best of your ability.

You Struggle to Pitch Well in a Baseball Game

Do BRAAD to stop egoic reactions when struggling to pitch well during a baseball game.

Egoic Reaction

You hold the egoic belief that you must "believe in yourself" to pitch well, so struggling to believe in yourself triggers egoic thinking.

1. **Egoic Thinking.** You have egoic defining and worrying thoughts like, "I don't believe in myself anymore. What will everyone think of me?"

2. **Egoic Emotions.** These thoughts trigger fear. Egoic pain intensifies your fear.

Awareness Moment

As you notice the fear, you realize your ego is active. You decide to do BRAAD to stop the egoic cycle and become AWACCE.

BRAAD in Action

1. **Breathe.** You take a slow, deep breath to stop the egoic cycle and release your emotions.

2. **Refocus.** You reset your focus to executing each pitch.

3. **Accept.** You accept how you've performed so far and your egoic reaction.

4. **Adjust.** You identify an adjustment: paying attention to your pitching mechanics for the next pitch.

5. **Do.** You implement this adjustment with intense awareness and acceptance.

Benefits of BRAAD

Doing BRAAD stops the egoic cycle, which:

1. Stops the egoic thinking and fear that makes pitching difficult.

2. Weakens your ego by not reinforcing the egoic belief that you must believe in yourself to perform well.

3. Strengthens your awareness and acceptance, allowing you to pitch more effectively.

You Argue with a Fan

Do BRAAD to stop egoic reactions when a fan is being disrespectful.

Egoic Reaction

You have an egoic belief that if someone disrespects you, you must retaliate, so the fan's disrespect triggers egoic thinking.

1. **Egoic Thinking.** You have egoic wanting and complaining thoughts like, "I have to shut that guy up! He shouldn't be talking to me like that!"

2. **Egoic Emotion.** These thoughts trigger anger. Egoic pain intensifies your anger.

3. **Egoic Action.** Driven by your egoic thoughts and emotions, you yell at the fan.

Awareness Moment

As you yell at the fan, you realize your ego is active. You decide to do BRAAD to stop the egoic cycle and become AWACCE.

BRAAD in Action

1. **Breathe.** You take a slow, deep breath to stop the egoic cycle and release your emotions.

2. **Refocus.** You reset your focus to playing basketball.

3. **Accept.** You accept your egoic reaction and the fact that the fan said something disrespectful.

4. **Adjust.** You identify adjustments: stop yelling and return your attention to playing the game.

5. **Do.** You implement these adjustments with intense awareness and acceptance.

Benefits of BRAAD

Doing BRAAD stops the egoic cycle, which:

1. Stops the egoic thinking and anger that drive you to yell at a fan.

2. Weakens your ego by not reinforcing the egoic belief that you must retaliate when disrespected.

3. Strengthens your awareness and acceptance, allowing you to play at your best.

You Want to Prove Your Critics Wrong

Do BRAAD to stop egoic reactions when you feel you must prove your critics wrong.

Egoic Reaction

You base your identity and worth on how people perceive you as a golfer, so hearing sports commentators doubt your abilities triggers egoic thinking.

1. **Egoic Thinking.** You have egoic wanting thoughts like, "I have to win to prove them wrong. Maybe I should cheat to guarantee a win."

2. **Egoic Emotion.** These thoughts trigger feelings of fear. Egoic pain intensifies your fear.

Awareness Moment

As you contemplate cheating, you realize your ego is active. You decide to do BRAAD to stop the egoic cycle and become AWACCE.

BRAAD in Action

1. **Breathe.** You take a slow, deep breath to stop the egoic cycle and release your emotions.

2. **Refocus.** You reset your focus to playing golf.

3. **Accept.** You accept your egoic reaction and what the sports commentators are saying.

4. **Adjust.** You identify an adjustment: pay attention to each golf shot.

5. **Do.** You implement this adjustment with intense awareness and acceptance.

Benefits of BRAAD

Doing BRAAD stops the egoic cycle, which:

1. Stops the egoic wanting and fear that drive you to want to cheat.

2. Weakens your ego by not reinforcing that your identity and worth depend on others' perceptions of you.

3. Strengthens your awareness and acceptance, allowing you to compete fearlessly.

Stuck in the Past

You Dwell on Your Ex-Husband

Do BRAAD to stop egoic reactions while catching up on your favorite TV show.

Egoic Reaction

You haven't accepted the experience of your last relationship, so when the pain surfaces, it triggers egoic thinking.

1. **Egoic Thinking.** You have egoic ruminating thoughts like, "He ruined our relationship. I wasted my time. I was mistreated."

2. **Egoic Emotion.** These thoughts trigger anger. Egoic pain intensifies the anger.

3. **Egoic Action.** Driven by your egoic thoughts and emotions, you start eating junk food to feel better.

Awareness Moment

As you start eating junk food, you realize your ego is active. You decide to do BRAAD to stop the egoic cycle and become AWACCE.

BRAAD in Action

1. **Breathe.** You take a slow, deep breath to stop the egoic cycle and release your emotions.

2. **Refocus.** You reset your focus to watching your favorite TV show.

3. **Accept.** You accept that you were ruminating about your past relationship.

4. **Adjust.** You identify adjustments: stop eating the junk food, watch your TV show, and do the Forgive the Past exercise tomorrow morning.

5. **Do.** You implement these adjustments with intense awareness and acceptance.

Benefits of BRAAD

Doing BRAAD stops the egoic cycle, which:

1. Stops the ruminating and anger that drive you to eat junk food.

2. Weakens your ego by not reinforcing thoughts about your past relationship.

3. Strengthens your awareness and acceptance, allowing you to enjoy your favorite TV show.

You Ruminate About Your Unhappy Childhood

Do BRAAD to stop egoic reactions when ruminating about your childhood.

Egoic Reaction

You haven't accepted your unhappy childhood, so when the pain from it surfaces, it triggers egoic thinking.

1. **Egoic Thinking.** You have egoic ruminating thoughts like, "Why were my parents so harsh? They never let me be a kid. They were cruel and unloving."

2. **Egoic Emotion.** These thoughts trigger sadness. Egoic pain intensifies these emotions.

3. **Egoic Action.** Driven by your egoic thoughts and emotions, you distract yourself to avoid facing the past.

Awareness Moment

As you notice you're avoiding your past, you recognize your ego is active. You decide to do BRAAD to stop the egoic cycle and become AWACCE.

BRAAD in Action

1. **Breathe.** You take a slow, deep breath to stop the egoic cycle and release your emotions.

2. **Refocus.** You reset your focus to releasing the past.

3. **Accept.** You accept your egoic reaction and that your childhood can't be changed.

4. **Adjust.** You identify an adjustment: to do the Forgive the Past exercise.

5. **Do.** You implement this adjustment with intense awareness and acceptance.

Benefits of BRAAD

Doing BRAAD stops the egoic cycle, which:

1. Stops the ruminating thoughts and sadness that prolong unnecessary suffering.

2. Weakens your ego by not reinforcing thoughts about your unhappy childhood.

3. Strengthens your awareness and acceptance, allowing you to let go of past experiences.

Your Ex-Girlfriend Posts About Her New Relationship

Do BRAAD to stop egoic reactions when you see your ex-girlfriend in a new relationship on social media.

Egoic Reaction

Your happiness depends on feeling more successful in relationships than your ex-girlfriend, so seeing her in a new relationship triggers egoic thinking.

1. **Egoic Thinking.** You have egoic wanting thoughts like, "I hope their relationship crashes and burns. I should be the one who's happy and moving on!"

2. **Egoic Emotion.** These thoughts trigger bitterness. Egoic pain intensifies your bitterness.

3. **Egoic Action.** Driven by your egoic thoughts and emotions, you comment negatively on her social media post.

Awareness Moment

Before posting the comment, you realize your ego is active. You decide to do BRAAD to stop the egoic cycle and become AWACCE.

BRAAD in Action

1. **Breathe.** You take a slow, deep breath to stop the egoic cycle and release your emotions.

2. **Refocus.** You reset your focus to moving forward.

3. **Accept.** You accept your egoic reaction and that your ex-girlfriend is in a new relationship.

4. **Adjust.** You identify adjustments: delete the comment, close social media, and practice the Open to New Experiences exercise.

5. **Do.** You implement these adjustments with intense awareness and acceptance.

Benefits of BRAAD

Doing BRAAD stops the egoic cycle, which:

1. Stops the egoic wanting and bitterness that creates unnecessary suffering.

2. Weakens your ego by not reinforcing that your happiness depends on feeling more successful than your ex-girlfriend.

3. Strengthens your awareness and acceptance, allowing you to let go of relationships that are over.

Shopping

You Shop to Fill an Emotional Void

Do BRAAD to stop egoic reactions when you're shopping to fill emptiness.

Egoic Reaction

You shop to feel happy and avoid feeling empty. Feeling emptiness triggers egoic thinking.

1. **Egoic Thinking.** You have egoic wanting thoughts like, "I need something new to fill this void."

2. **Egoic Emotion.** These thoughts trigger strong desire.

3. **Egoic Action.** Driven by your egoic thoughts and emotions, you impulsively purchase something online.

Awareness Moment

After hitting the buy button, you realize your ego is active. You decide to do BRAAD to stop the egoic cycle and become AWACCE.

BRAAD in Action

1. **Breathe.** You take a slow, deep breath to stop the egoic cycle and release your emotions.

2. **Refocus.** You reset your focus to feeling your inner happiness.

3. **Accept.** You accept your egoic reaction.

4. **Adjust.** You identify adjustments: close the shopping app and practice the Inner Self Awareness exercise.

5. **Do.** You implement these adjustments with intense awareness and acceptance.

Benefits of BRAAD

Doing BRAAD stops the egoic cycle, which:

1. Stops the egoic thinking and desire that drive you to shop.

2. Weakens your ego by not reinforcing that your happiness depends on buying new things.

3. Strengthens your awareness and acceptance, allowing you to feel inner happiness.

You Buy Expensive Suits to Feel Important

Do BRAAD to stop egoic reactions that drive you to buy suits to feel important.

Egoic Reaction

You base your identity and worth on feeling important. Buying expensive suits makes you feel important, and the fear of being seen as a "nobody" triggers egoic thinking.

1. **Egoic Thinking.** You have egoic wanting and worrying thoughts like, "I need a new expensive suit. I'm worried people will discover I'm a nobody."

2. **Egoic Emotion.** These thoughts trigger feelings of fear. Egoic pain intensifies your fear.

Awareness Moment

As you're about to leave for the store, you realize your ego is active. You decide to do BRAAD to stop the egoic cycle and become AWACCE.

BRAAD in Action

1. **Breathe.** You take a slow, deep breath to stop the egoic cycle and release your emotions.

2. **Refocus.** You reset your focus to taking your dog for a walk.

3. **Accept.** You accept your egoic reaction.

4. **Adjust.** You identify an adjustment: take your dog for a walk.

5. **Do.** You implement this adjustment with intense awareness and acceptance.

Benefits of BRAAD

Doing BRAAD stops the egoic cycle, which:

1. Stops the egoic thinking and fear that drive you to shop.

2. Weakens your ego by not reinforcing that your identity and worth depend on expensive suits.

3. Strengthens your awareness and acceptance, allowing you to make decisions not driven by the ego.

Vacation

Your Vacation Is Almost Over

Do BRAAD to stop egoic reactions when your vacation is coming to an end.

Egoic Reaction

You base your happiness on being on vacation, so thinking about your vacation ending triggers egoic thinking.

1. **Egoic Thinking.** You have egoic complaining thoughts like, "I don't want my vacation to end! Why can't it last longer?"

2. **Egoic Emotion.** These thoughts trigger sadness. Egoic pain intensifies your sadness.

3. **Egoic Action.** Driven by your egoic thoughts and emotions, you start drinking excessively to numb your sadness.

Awareness Moment

The next morning, you wake up slightly hungover and notice you're still complaining, which makes you realize your ego is active. You decide to do BRAAD to stop egoic thinking and become AWACCE.

BRAAD in Action

1. **Breathe.** You take a slow, deep breath to interrupt egoic thinking and release your emotions.

2. **Refocus.** You reset your focus to enjoying your vacation.

3. **Accept.** You accept your egoic reaction and that your vacation will soon end.

4. **Adjust.** You identify adjustments: go swimming and do BRAAD when egoic thinking starts again.

5. **Do.** You implement these adjustments with intense awareness and acceptance.

Benefits of BRAAD

Doing BRAAD stops the egoic cycle, which:

1. Stops the egoic complaining and sadness from ruining your vacation.

2. Weakens your ego by not reinforcing that your happiness depends on vacation.

3. Strengthens your awareness and acceptance, allowing you to enjoy your vacation.

Be agile in life by being AWACCE—
AWareness and ACCEptance.

7. FAQS

How do I know when my focus is egoic?

The focus of an experience is egoic when it supports one or more parts of the ego.

- **Egoic Identity** - Your focus is to enhance or protect your sense of self.

- **Egoic Worth** - Your focus is to enhance or protect your worth.

- **Egoic Happiness** - Your focus is to fill emptiness using something external.

- **Egoic Past and Pain** - Your focus is on an experience you haven't accepted.

- **Egoic Future** - Your focus is on a possible future experience you fear.

- **Egoic Beliefs** - Your focus is associated with a belief you would never consider changing.

How am I supposed to be aware of many things simultaneously, like what I'm seeing, hearing, and doing?

Each experience is a series of multiple moments. In each moment, you will be aware of one thing and then switch to being aware of another in the next moment. So, over an entire experience, you are switching what you are aware of depending on the experience's focus and what's happening in the moment.

Does being AWACCE mean I can't be ambitious?

No. Ambition is not inherently egoic. It is only egoic when it aligns with a part of your ego.

- **Egoic Identity** - You want to win to maintain or achieve a new identity.

- **Egoic Worth** - You want to win to feel worthy.

- **Egoic Happiness** - You want to win to replace emptiness.

Does being AWACCE mean I can't think about the past?

No. When an experience requires thinking about the past, you think about the past intentionally.

Does being AWACCE mean I can't think about the future?

No. When an experience requires thinking about the future, you think about the future intentionally.

Does being AWACCE mean I shouldn't prepare for the future?

No. Being AWACCE means being in a state of awareness and acceptance. It doesn't mean to avoid the practicalities of life, such as preparing for the future.

Does being AWACCE mean everything will be easy and that I will always be happy?

Being AWACCE doesn't mean life will be easy or you'll never experience unhappiness. Life is hard. You'll face challenges and feel unhappy sometimes, just like everyone else. But you'll approach challenges responsively, with intense focus and the full power of your mind. You'll recognize unhappiness and external happiness as temporary experiences, allowing them to come and go without resistance. Beneath every challenging experience, you'll still feel a deep inner happiness (i.e., inner peace), making tough times easier to handle.

Are thinking and awareness the same thing?

No. Thinking is an activity of the mind. Awareness is an activity of the conscious self.

Are all emotions egoic?

No. Emotions created from egoic thinking are egoic. Emotions that result from your response to an experience are not egoic.

Be agile in life by being AWACCE—
AWareness and ACCEptance.

WANT MORE?

Thanks for reading! Visit our website, egozero.co, to explore additional offerings.

You'll find courses, downloads, and much more!

Visit us today: egozero.co

Be agile in life by being AWACCE—
AWareness and ACCEptance.

Made in United States
North Haven, CT
03 August 2025

71291506R00098